About the Author

Gail Seekamp is personal finance editor at *The Sunday Business Post*, and has written about consumer finance topics for over seven years. She has worked as a journalist in Mexico City, London and Dublin for fifteen years and is a graduate of Sussex University. She won the 1996 ESB National Media Award in Business and Financial Journalism.

The Woman's Guide to
Personal Finance

Gail Seekamp

Oak Tree Press
Dublin

Dedication:
To the most patient of men

A catalogue record of this book is
available from the British Library.

ISBN 1-86076-051-1

Oak Tree Press
Merrion Building
Lower Merrion Street
Dublin 2, Ireland

Printed in Ireland by Colour Books Ltd.

Every effort has been made to ensure the accuracy of the contents of this
book, including updated information from the 1997 Budget. However,
changes in tax and Social Welfare may be introduced in the Finance and
Social Welfare Bills later in the year. Neither the publisher nor the author
can be held liable for any errors or omissions nor for any action taken as
a result of information in this book. Readers are advised to take professional advice, where appropriate

Contents

PART 1: MONEY MANAGEMENT

PART 2: LIFE-CYCLE PLANNING

Acknowledgements

I owe a debt of gratitude and thanks to many people. Without their help, this book would not exist.

Firstly to Brian O'Kane, managing director of Oak Tree Press, who dreamed up the idea. Both he and general manager David Givens also supported and guided the project in a very busy period. My thanks also to *The Sunday Business Post*, in particular to Aileen O'Toole, deputy editor, and Fiachra O'Riordan, marketing manager, who also gave generous backing when deadlines were tight.

At a professional level, many others gave vital help. Particular thanks are due to Pam Kearney, partner in O'Hare & Associates (chartered accountants), who provided tax data for the Child Care chapter in the hectic days before January 31. Kathy Dillon, co-founder of LifeWise, the Dublin insurance brokerage that specialises in financial planning for women, gave examples for the Protection and Pension chapters. Fiona Duffy of Brian Phelan & Co accountants helped provide information for the Flexi-work chapter as did Mike Murphy Insurances with the familiar warning — shop around!

Jim Ryan, senior tax manager at Ernst & Young's personal financial services division, helped check Chapter 17, and Brian Bohan, now at Bohan Solicitors, lent his knowledge of inheritance planning once again. Eugene Davy and Rosemary Horgan, both family law solicitors, helped clarify issues relating to marital breakdown, A & L Goodbody (solicitors) provided information on wills, and Hilary Walpole, legal expert at Craig Gardner, Cork, kindly verified Chapter 12.

My thanks to those who dug out useful data on women, including Eilis O'Brien of Bank of Ireland, Irish Life's Ray Gordon, Anne

Mathews at Norwich Union and Ita Gibney. Carmel Foley, chief executive of the Employment Equality Agency, EEA information officer Kathleen Connolly, and Veronica Scanlan, Department of Social Welfare press office, also gave valuable help.

Others deserve a mention and thanks, including the press offices of the Revenue Commissioners, Department of Finance, FAS. Acknowledgments also to BDO Simpson Xavier, BZW, Davy Stockbrokers', FAS and *The Sunday Business Post* for material reproduced in the book.

Warm thanks are due to Bride Rosney, special advisor to the President at Aras an Uachtarain, Mary Russell and Eithne Strong who gave permission for quotes used in the book.

Sandra Hayes, production manager at Oak Tree Press, added greatly to the book's appearance, as did colleagues Brian, Anne-Marie, Marian and cartoonist John Leonard.

At a personal level, many thanks to the friends who suggested improvements and quotes, especially Aisling, Josiane, Anne and Maura O'Carroll, Ann, Marion, Carole and Nora. Finally, to Stephen, for his sterling work, and Pierce, who gave unstinting support — and many insights — in recent weeks.

All the above contributed greatly. Any mistakes that remain are my own responsibility, not theirs.

Gail Seekamp, February 1997

How to Use this Book

"A man thinks he knows, but a woman knows better."

Chinese Proverb

Do women need a book on personal finance? Yes, is the short answer.

Here's why. Statistically, you will live longer, earn less and take more career breaks than the average man, for starters. If children arrive, you're far more likely to leave your job or start working part-time than your male partner. That means, over your lifetime, you'll probably earn less than Mr Average, but must stretch your money further.

Take your company pension scheme. You've got to invest more to get the same pension at retirement as a man, because you will draw on this nest egg — in theory — for a few years longer. Furthermore, 92 per cent of Irish housewives have never belonged to a company scheme. Many won't qualify for a full State Contributory pension either, because they don't have enough PRSI credits.

Some of these women face a bleak retirement unless they act, now.

There's good news, too. We are catching up at school, college and in the workplace and have more spending power, independence and — hopefully — confidence than ever before. Girls got better grades at the higher level Leaving Cert than boys in 1994, and almost half the undergraduate places at college, RTCs and universities that Autumn. Women took a startling 73 per cent of all "new" jobs created in the year up to April 1996, most of them in the services sector.

Thanks to promotion and equality legislation, the wage gap is closing. Women in industry earned 57 per cent of the average male hourly wage in 1971, rising to 69 per cent in 1995. In the broader economy, women now earn 80 per cent of the typical male salary.

Meanwhile, other social factors are creating opportunities and pitfalls for women of all ages. They are marrying later and having less children now, but their marriage is less likely to last.

How can this book help?

Women *are* clued in about money, perhaps more so than men. Eagle Star's 1996 "Family Finances Survey" found that while 90 per cent of married couples in the UK make joint decisions about money, the man's decision was often based on his wife's advice. When quizzed on the impact of divorce on the main bread-winner's pension, 34 per cent of men did not know that their own pension could be divided. Only 16 per cent of the women hadn't realised this.

But women need concise, accurate information, without being patronised, to help them tackle issues like: which mortgage, or pension plan should I choose? Can I job-share after my baby is born? Where can I invest, safely?

This is a book to dip into. Like *Personal Finance 1996/97*, it takes a needs-driven approach which looks at key "tasks", like investing or buying a house. But it's tailored for your personal and family needs. *The Woman's Guide to Personal Finance* is divided into three sections and more clearly sign-posted, to help you find information quickly.

Part One looks at money management. Tackling the first task — your own financial "audit" — will reveal a lot about your needs. Why not try it first?

PART 1: "TASK" CHECKLIST

- Do a financial audit   p. 6
- Picking a current account   p. 10
- Saving safely   p. 26
- Buying a house   p. 50
- Borrowing   p. 37
- Protecting your family and possessions   p. 76

You may prefer a more holistic, or integrated, approach. Needs can shift as you get older, or your family circumstances change, so the middle section of this book looks at "life-cycle" planning. These chapters deal with "life-issues", rather than specific "tasks".

PART 2: "LIFE-CYCLE" CHECKLIST

- Love and marriage   p. 120
- Having a child   p. 130
- Separation and divorce   p. 148

Part Three covers Future Planning. It looks at issues like this:

PART 3: "FUTURE PLANNING" CHECKLIST

- Starting your own business   p. 176
- Pension planning   p. 183
- Sorting out tax   p. 200
- Investing for Profit   p. 215
- Inheritance planning   p. 232

You can also dip into *The Woman's Guide to Personal Finance* for information on a specific tax, financial product, etc. Want to know the return on An Post's Savings Certs, or read up on pension mortgages? Turn to the index (p. 267). There's also a glossary (p. 263) and an Appendix (p. 247), with more information and other sources of advice.

Back to men, or rather women and men. Many women now have their own bank account, credit card, mortgage and separate pension plan. This growing financial independence is healthy. But there's a strong case for joint planning by a woman and her partner, especially if they co-habit, marry and/or have a child. This book is for women *and* all the important people in their lives.

Part 1

Money Management

1

Starting to Plan

"We live in a time of enormous change, advance and challenge for women."

President Mary Robinson in her opening address to the
Global Forum of Women, Dublin 1992

Let's start with the basics: doing a "financial audit" of yourself. Think of your personal or family budget as if you were running a small business. The trick is to boost income (by earning better returns on savings, claiming tax allowances, etc.) and cut expenditure (reduce bank charges, insurance costs, etc.). But you must *know* what you are spending before you start to plan.

Jot down a personal profile of yourself, like the one below:

PERSONAL PROFILE

Name:	Mary McNamara
Age:	28
Marital Status:	Married
Children:	Joe (5 years), Maire (3 years)
Job status:	Part-time worker
Top tax rate:	26%
Plans:	Marketing diploma, sun holiday, etc.

Now, do a monthly budget that lists your personal/family income and expenditure:

YOUR MONTHLY OUTGOINGS

Home Bills		
	Electricity	£
	Gas	£
	Other Heating	£
	Telephone	£
	House Insurance	£
	Water/Refuse/Rates/Service Charges	£
Other Costs		
	VHI (or other medical insurance)	£
	TV (licence, rental, repayments)	£
	Holiday Expenses	£
	Entertainment Expenses	£
	Sports/Hobbies/Clubs	£
	Food, Household Items	£
	Fares to Work	£
	Clothing	£
Car(s) etc.		
	Road Tax	£
	Insurance	£
	Petrol	£
	Repairs etc.	£
Miscellaneous, e.g.		
	Savings/Investment Plans etc.	£
	Life Assurance etc.	£
	Other	£
Credit Commitments		
	Mortgage	£
	Car Loan	£
	Washing Machine etc.	£
	Credit Card	£
	Store Cards	£
Total Monthly Costs		£

Your Monthly Income

Salary (after tax and other deductions)	£
Guaranteed Overtime/Bonus (after tax etc.)	£
Payments/Commission	£
Income from Savings	£
Partner's Salary (after tax etc.)	£
Partner's Guaranteed Overtime/Bonus (after tax etc.)	£
Partner's Payments/Commission	£
Partner's Income from Savings	£
Social Welfare Payments, e.g. Child Benefit	£
Total Monthly Income	£
Total Monthly Costs	£
Balance	£

Work out what you (and your partner, if appropriate) spend each month. Does it match your income? Is there any spare cash left? Can you spend less?

Next, use the personal and budgetary data to do a financial audit or "health check", as it's also called, as in this example:

FINANCIAL AUDIT

1. Do I have short-term loans (overdraft, credit card, etc.)? Can I borrow cheaply?

2. Can I get a cheaper mortgage?

3. Do I have any investments? Are they safe and earning a high rate of interest? Have I lost track of any (savings account lodgement book, etc.)?

4. Do I have an emergency "nest egg" in a bank, building society or Post Office?

5. Can I start a regular savings plan, or lock up a lump sum for the future (pre-retirement)?

6. Am I saving for a pension? Is it enough?

7. Do I (and my partner) have insurance to protect our incomes if we fall sick, lose our jobs or even die? Is my house/car insurance good value?

8. Do I (and my partner) have an up-to-date will? Should we think about inheritance planning?

9. Am I claiming all the tax allowances and social welfare benefits I'm entitled to?

In answering these or similar questions, you pin-point the weaknesses in your budget, and clarify your key needs (see Contents for "tasks"). A good financial adviser should do a similar exercise before selling a product or service. If he/she doesn't, you already have!

In the example above, Mary might start saving with the Post Office, join her company pension scheme and take out life assurance for her family's sake.

Simple changes can be more lasting than bold ones. Before buying company shares for grandchildren (not yet born!), try to get more value from your current income.

MONEY MANAGEMENT: THE BASIC TOOLS

- A well-chosen current account   p. 10
- Other account options   p. 11
- Household budget scheme   p. 18

Current Account

This is a place where you can store money, pay bills, cash cheques, etc. Most people have their salary or other income paid directly into their account, and withdraw cash as they need it. You usually get a chequebook as part of the package (unless you are a student), plus a cheque guarantee card which allows you to cash cheques of up to £100. Current account holders also get a plastic card for withdrawing cash from the "hole in the wall" (the Automated Teller Machine — ATM).

There are four associated banks in Ireland — AIB Bank, Bank of Ireland (BoI), National Irish Bank and Ulster Bank — and the vast majority of current account holders bank with one of these institutions. The associated banks have far more ATMs than the building societies, almost 900 in total. This gives you better access to your money. Furthermore, banks normally give overdraft facilities to clients who need to borrow money for a short while (see also Chapter 4). Building societies do not.

Bank-based current accounts also help you to build a commercial relationship with your bank manager, which may give you access to a cheaper mortgage in the future or gentler treatment if you get into financial difficulty. But you have to run the account well, and not have a history of unauthorised overdrafts.

These accounts have drawbacks. It's hard to avoid bank charges, unless you keep a certain sum in the account each month (see "How Do They Compare?" table on pp. 15–16). Also, they rarely pay interest on credit balances, and are a bad place for parking large sums of cash.

Associated Banks/Interest-Bearing Current Accounts

All four banks, as well as giving you a cheque book, also offer current accounts that pay interest on credit balances, but the rewards are small, and the conditions strict. See table on following page for a comparison.

Associated Banks/Deposit Account

This is a poor third choice. Some accounts allow you to withdraw funds with an ATM card, instead of via a "passbook" (deposit book). Ordinary bank deposit accounts pay very little interest on your balance, and Deposit Interest Retention Tax (DIRT) is deducted too (now 26 per cent).

You can pay bills, for a fee, but get no chequebook.

Other Options

ACCBANK/Current Account

This is an ordinary current account, with chequebook and cheque guarantee card. It pays low interest on balances, and has ATM access (ACCBANK & BoI). If you do not need a cheque guarantee card or overdraft, ACCBANK's Cheque Save has no quarterly charge.

COMPARISON OF INTEREST BEARING CURRENT ACCOUNTS

Institution	Product	Restrictions	Interest Paid	Other Benefits
AIB Bank	Credit Interest Account	No overdraft/ ATM Card. £300 min. opening balance.	0.25% on all balances.	Chequebook, cheque guarantee card and Euro-cheque facility.
Bank of Ireland	Ascent	Under 25s only.	1.75%–2.25% depending on balance.	As per current account. Low-cost. No transaction charges.
National Irish Bank	Freebank	No overdraft.	1.25% on all balances	No transaction charges*, see pp. 15-16.
Ulster Bank	Premium	£2,500 min. balance to earn premium interest. No overdraft.	1%–2% depending on balance.	Chequebook transactions, own charge structure.

* Privilege Account has higher rates for over 45s.

Source: Institutions listed.

Budget Accounts

The main banks offer accounts that help to spread costs throughout the year and enable you to pay big bills, such as your car or household insurance. They all work on the same principle, by adding up your annual bills, adding a bit for inflation, and dividing by 12. You then arrange for this sum to be transferred into your budget account each month (usually from your current account).

This account is for paying bills. You can make payments with a chequebook, standing order or a direct debit facility. The account may go into the red if you make a large payment, but you'll have a credit balance at other times.

Banks usually charge a small quarterly fee for these accounts, plus an interest penalty during the months when you have to "borrow" money, and they may not pay interest on credit balances.

Credit Union/Share (Deposit) Account

This will probably supplement, not replace, an ordinary current or deposit account. However, it may be possible to have a full current account with some credit unions soon.

Credit unions are co-operative and community-based, and open to people who live in one geographic area or are united by another common bond, such as membership of a trade union or company. Pending new legislation, which may allow them to offer current accounts, credit unions give their members access to cheap loans (see Chapter 4). Some also have bill-paying facilities, provide cut-price home insurance and VHI premiums. A tiny few allow ATM access.

Irish Permanent/Current Account

A fully-fledged bank since 1994, the Irish Permanent offers four current accounts. Each offers a slightly different package, in terms of services, fees and interest yield. Irish Permanent shares its ATMs with Bank of Ireland, so customers can access about 400 machines.

Merchant, Investment and Private Banks/Current Account

AIB Bank, Bank of Ireland and Guinness & Mahon offer a full banking service for rich people. Called "private banking", this includes extra facilities, investment advice, etc. Other merchant/investment banks like ABN Amro do not have current accounts but offer deposit-taking and advice services.

Post Office/Savings Account

You can open a regular account at the Post Office Savings Bank. The interest rate depends on the credit balance in the account, but starts at 0.5 per cent (deposits up to £5,000) before DIRT is deducted.

You can pay a range of bills, including the TV licence, local authority bills, gas bill, and telephone bill, through Bill Pay. People who are living on social welfare payments can also pay bills directly through the Household Budget scheme (see p. 18). The Post Office has long opening hours — 9.00 a.m. to 5.30 p.m. at most main branches — but no ATM network.

TSB/Current Account

TSB Bank offers mortgages, personal loans, a chequebook facility and access to ATMs. It also has longer opening hours than the main associated banks, but lower transaction charges. TSB Bank shares its ATM network with AIB, Ulster Bank and BoI. From March 1997, customers will be able to access over 1,100 ATMs.

TIP: If you want an easy way to pay for Shopping, get a Laser card with your current account. It's a payment card that works like an electronic cheque. See also p. 19

WHICH ONE TO CHOOSE?

That depends on your needs. If you already have a current account, look at your bank statement and check what bank services you are now using — such as a standing order or direct debit, for example. Are you paying charges? If so, how much?

BANK CHARGES

Because of the convenience factor, most people end up choosing a bank-based current account. Here's a list of the charges that applied in January 1997:

How Do They Compare?

Transaction	AIB	BoI	NIB	Ulster	ACC	IP	TSB
ATM Withdrawal/ Deposit*	17p	19p	15p	18p	20p	Nil	10p[†]
Cheque Card	£3	£3.15	£5[‡]	£3[‡]	£2.50	Nil	£2.50
Direct Debit (set up)	Nil	£2.70	£2.50	£2.50	£2	Nil	£2.50
Direct Debit (transaction fee)	17p	19p	15p	18p	15p	Nil	15p
Paper Withdrawal/ Deposit	24p	26p/22p	24p	25p/24p	22p	Nil	23p
Standing Order (set up)	£3	£2.70	£3	£3	£2	Nil	£2.50
Standing Order (transaction fee)	29p	31p	27p	37p	30p	Nil	30p
Statement	Nil	Nil	Nil	Nil	Nil	Nil	Nil
Quarterly Fee	£3.75**	£4.15[††]	£3.75	£3.90	£3	£10[‡‡]	£3

* Not all banks have a deposit facility on their ATMs.

† From TSB Bank's own ATMs. 20p charge for transactions on other bank's ATMs.

‡ Fee charged every two years.

** If you also want an overdraft facility with a chequebook, AIB charges an extra £20 annual fee, on top of the transaction charges listed above. If you want an overdraft facility but no chequebook (called an "on line" overdraft) there is a fixed £12 quarterly fee, but no transaction charges.

†† BoI also charges an annual £20 fee, on top of the quarterly and transaction fees, for standard customers who want an overdraft.

‡‡ All details are for IP's Merit Account. It also pays interest at 0.7% gross (£1–£999), or 1.25% (£1,000+).

Key: ACC = ACCBANK; AIB = AIB Bank; BoI = Bank of Ireland; IP = Irish Permanent; NIB = National Irish Bank; TSB = TSB Bank; Ulster = Ulster Bank.

Source: Institutions listed. Comparisons based on ordinary current accounts offered by main banks only.

Free Banking

If you meet certain conditions, your bank will waive the quarterly fee and most transaction charges. This is called "free banking", but you still have to pay some charges, such as the cheque-card fee, standing-order set-up charge and £5 yearly government stamp duty on ATM card. The conditions for "Free Banking" are listed below.

THE CONDITIONS FOR "FREE BANKING"

Bank	Conditions
AIB	Customers who keep a minimum £100 balance in the account during the quarter. Also, customers who have their salaries paid directly into the account via the "PayPath" scheme (charges waived for the first 18 months only); full-time students in credit, "One to One" customers (60+, widowed, visually impaired) and some others. Ask at the bank.
BoI	Minimum £100 balance during the quarter, also customers who have their salaries paid directly into the account via "PayPath" for the first 18 months, students and "Golden Years" (elderly) customers.
NIB	Customers who remain in credit for the charging quarter, Freebank customers, and those paid direct via "Safepay" (18 months).
Ulster	Customers who remain in credit for charging quarter and "Paypath" customers.
ACC	Does not offer "free banking". However, it pays interest on daily credit balances over £200.
IP	Only the over 60s and "Prestige" account customers qualify for "free banking". The latter need a £5,000 minimum balance.
TSB	Customers who keep a minimum cleared £100 balance or, if the balance dips below that, an average cleared balance of £300 throughout the quarter. Also, "PayPath" customers (first 18 months), students and the over 60s.

The next time you are in your bank, ask for a leaflet about bank charges and find out if there are other products with lower charges.

Or, pick a bank which only charges you when you slip into the red. Don't ask for an overdraft facility or, if you do, try to clear it within three months.

Here's what a typical customer pays:

> *Joan has an account at a leading bank. She writes about five cheques a month, and uses the ATM machine four times a week, on average. She has two direct debits on her account for the mortgage payment and mortgage protection policy, and a standing order for a life assurance payment. Joan's account balance usually drops to a few pounds at the end of each month, so she doesn't qualify for free banking at her bank. This is what her bill looks like after one year:*
>
> | Service | Annual Fee |
> |---|---|
> | *60 cheques* | £14.40 |
> | *208 ATM transactions* | £35.36 |
> | *24 direct debits* | £4.08 |
> | *12 standing orders* | £3.48* |
> | *4 quarterly fees* | £15.00 |
> | *Total* | £72.32 |
>
> ** This includes the bank's own charge of £2.04 (17p x 12), plus a £1.44 fee (12p x 12p) which would be levied regardless of whether or not Joan qualified for "free banking".*
>
> *Joan might feel that £72.32 is a small sum to pay for a full banking service. But she could get the same service elsewhere for just £1.44 (the standing order fee) if she switched to a bank that offered "free banking". If she asks for an overdraft, the cost will rise by another £20 per year.*

CHECKING YOUR ACCOUNT

It pays to examine your bank statement very closely. Bank clerks make errors, just like every other human being and you may be charged too much interest on a loan as a result. Several companies offer statement checking services which can spot overcharging. If you have any problem with your bank or building society over a current or deposit account, talk to that institution's customer services department. If that fails, contact the Ombudsman for the Credit Institutions, 8 Adelaide Court, Dublin 2 (Tel: (01) 478 3755).

Joint Account

Do you want a joint account with your partner, or an account in your own name? This issue is covered on p. 121. A joint account with a single signature authority gives both of you easy access to funds — not a good idea if your partner is a spendthrift!

Also, if you have a building society account in joint names, and that account qualifies you for a free share hand-out (in the event of the Society "going public") only the first-named person on the account will be entitled to shares. This will no longer apply if your partner dies before you, thanks to a rule change in the Central Bank Act 1996.

HOUSEHOLD BUDGET SCHEME

This facility is operated for the Department of Social Welfare by An Post. If you are getting unemployment benefit or assistance, you can arrange to pay certain bills by having money deducted from your welfare payments. The scheme covers the following:

- Local authority rents and mortgages

- ESB bills

- Gas bills

- Telephone bills.

You can only use the scheme if you're getting an unemployment payment and are being paid via the Postdraft method (at An Post). Only 25 per cent of your payment can be earmarked for direct payments. If the sum paid each week does not cover your bills, you're still liable to pay the balance.

Contact An Post's freephone number (1-800-707172) for details.

CONCLUSION

A financial audit is a good way to get your personal finances on track. It should focus your mind on a few key issues: namely, your budget (or lack of one); your needs; and how you are catering for them.

A critical look at your current account is also useful. Can you avoid bank charges and still get the level of service you need? Are you getting value for money? If not, consider the alternatives.

Don't forget the bigger picture either, and the reason why you bought this book!

- Personal financial planning can be viewed as a series of "tasks". You can solve a problem or achieve a certain goal by tackling each task.

- Be aware of your needs, and match these with a financial product — not vice versa.

- As a woman, your needs may change dramatically, so keep your plans flexible.

2

Why Save?

"What is a new bonnet, or a new pelisse (fur piece) to the pleasure of feeling there is something in reserve that you may call your own! Blessings on the Savings Bank!"

Hannah Farnham Lee (1780–1865), American author

Women need to save, but not just because we usually have babies and live longer than men. It's good for our self-esteem and creates a safety net in the event of sickness, divorce or other problems.

Thrift is old-fashioned but it's an excellent habit. Savings can pay for a holiday or pension. A nest egg can solve a short-term problem — being out of work for three months through sickness, for example — from spiralling into a crisis.

The next chapter looks at *safe* investment options. It covers regular savings (usually, a monthly contribution) and lump sum investments. Chapter 22 covers aggressive investments like equities and life assurance savings plans, aimed at long-term savers and high-income earners. These may put your capital at risk.

Instead of going to a bank, building society or insurance company and being "sold" a savings plan, think first:

- Why do I want to save?

- How much can I save?

- What other concerns do I have (inflation, risk, etc.)?

DEFINING NEEDS

Being clear about your goals makes it easier to pick a suitable product. Here's a list of typical savings targets:

Short Term (0–3 Years)	Mid-Term (3–10 Years)	Long Term (Over 10 Years)
Emergency Fund	Car	Pension
Holiday	Marriage	Children's future
Christmas	New Kitchen	
College Course	House Deposit	
Decorating Job	Big Trip	

Regardless of other plans, try to save a cash reserve — equal to three month's salary or more. Make this a top priority. Think like a squirrel!

Now, examine your budget (Chapter 1, pp 7–8), see how much you can afford to save, then begin. Saving is most painless when it's easy, so why not set up a direct debit from your wages? Or, if you have a family, save each £29 (£30 from Sept. 1997) monthly child benefit cheque with An Post?

To save successfully, match your savings term with a suitable product (see pp. 33–34). Over the long term (10 to 20 years), the average *yield* on shares outperforms the return on deposit accounts. But think about other issues, too:

Access to Cash

Don't lock up all your savings in a long-term home in case you need cash in a hurry. Insurance-based products — especially regular savings plans, where most of the first years' premiums can be absorbed in charges — can be liable to big "early encashment" penalties. An Post is a better option.

Keep your emergency fund in a safe home that isn't too accessible. Spread your cash. Aim for a portfolio that gives instant access to a large chunk of money, say three-quarters of your cash assets, but offers mid- and long-term gains as well.

Confidentiality

If you are a high-income earner or have brought cash back to Ireland on which you have never paid tax, this may concern you.

A product is "confidential" if the Revenue Commissioners (tax authorities) are not told about your investment. All of An Post's savings products are confidential, as are life assurance-based investment plans (unit-linked funds, etc.). But new legislation, aimed at curbing money laundering and other fraud, requires all financial institutions to question clients who suddenly deposit large cash sums.

Some low-tax products are not very confidential, such as:

- Special Savings Accounts (SSAs), see p. 29
- Special Investment Accounts (SIAs), see p. 223
- Business Expansion Schemes, see p. 226

Income

Some financial products pay all or part of the interest as an income, instead of a lump sum at the end. Income may be paid monthly, every three months (quarterly), half-yearly or annually, which may suit pensioners, for example.

Be careful. Ask if taking this income will eat into your capital, or if returns may change from year to year. Check if there are any charges and find out if they will eat into your income. (See Chapter 22, p. 230, for how to generate an income with An Post Savings Certs.)

Inflation

This erodes the buying power of your pound over time. If inflation averages 10 per cent per annum, your £10 will buy only £9 worth of goods after a year. Its nominal value will be the same, but its *real* value will have decreased.

The idea — albeit unlikely — that £1,000 may be worth just £57 in 2027 is shocking (see below). Clearly, any mid- or long-term investment product should at least keep pace with inflation. Bank and building society deposits often fail to do this, so you need to pick a more risky investment, like equities, which *may* grow faster than inflation over the long term.

REAL VALUE OF YOUR MONEY

Year	3% inflation	5% inflation	10% inflation
1997	£1,000	£1,000	£1,000
2007	£744	£614	£386
2017	£554	£377	£149
2027	£412	£231	£57

Source: Central Bank.

Risk/Reward

As a general rule, the return on an investment is inversely related to risk. That means, money which sits safely in a deposit account earns a low rate of interest. You can get double-digit returns on unit-linked funds, but may lose some capital if the stock market plunges. People close to retirement or on tight budgets can ill afford to take risks. More affluent people, and those saving over a longer term, can let time smooth out these short-term gains and losses.

The chart on the following page shows the *average* return on equities, gilts and cash over the past 20 years. It assumes that a person invested stg£1,000 on 31 December 1975.

VALUE OF £1,000 INVESTED ON 31/12/75, WITHDRAWN 31/12/95*

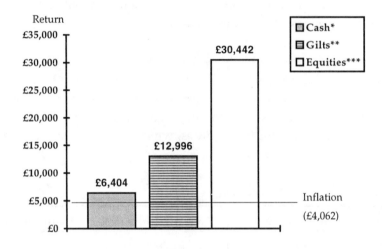

Notes: * This is a pre-tax value.
         ** Estimate of average building society yields.
         *** Based on FT All Share Index.
Source: BZW, London.

Strategy

Think strategically. If you are saving for a house, why not choose a bank or building society that offers a better mortgage rate for its own savers? This could save you a lot of money over a 20-year term.

Credit unions pay about 6 per cent interest on savings, and give members access to low-cost loans. They also discipline you into regular saving.

WARNING: Never take risks with capital you cannot afford to lose. Also, beware of investment advisers or financial institutions that offer spectacular gains. Your savings may not be safe. See Chapter 10 "How to Find *Good* Advice" p. 101.

Tax

Investment products are taxed in many ways, and some not at all. Most bank and building-society deposit accounts and life assurance-based investments (unit-linked funds and "with profits" funds — see Chapter 22), deduct 26 per cent tax from your profits. They pay the return *net* of tax. The tax rate on SSAs was increased from 10 per cent to 15 per cent in the 1995 Budget, but is still low. Many Post Office products are totally tax-free.

Other products pay returns *gross* of tax. You have to declare to the Revenue Commissioners any profit paid as a regular *income* or final *gain*. Make sure that you look at net (post-tax) returns when comparing products.

Top-rate taxpayers usually pay tax at 48 per cent on investment incomes, like interest from a foreign bank account. Profits taken when an investment is *encashed*, or *matures* — for example, equities — are usually liable for Capital Gains Tax (CGT). This tax, usually 40 per cent, is charged on the "profit" made on the difference between the purchase and sale price of the investment. You can make a yearly gain of £1,000 (£2,000 for married people) before paying CGT. There is a special 27 per cent CGT rate on some shares (see "Equities", Chapter 22). People who invest in equities through an SIA pay 10 per cent tax on all profits.

Put some cash in a tax-free or low-tax deposit, starting with An Post.

NOTE: People aged over 65 or permanently disabled do not have to pay DIRT on their savings. To claim a refund, fill out a form at the bank or building society and send it to the Revenue Commissioners.

3

Saving Safely

"He who hesitates is last."

Mae West (1982–1980), US actress

You've decided to save, *without* risking your money. Now what are your options? This chapter looks at these alternatives:

> - An Post: mid-term savings   p. 26
> - Bank/Building Society: Term,
>   Notice accounts, SSAs, Tracker Bonds   p. 28
> - Credit Union: for borrowers   p. 31
> - Government: Gilts for safety   p. 31
> - Life Insurance Companies:
>   Guaranteed bonds, Tracker bonds   p. 32

For "best" options for short- and mid-term savings, see pp. 33–34.

An Post

The Post Office is a very good choice for short- and mid-term savings. Returns fell in 1996, but they are still *tax-free* and *confidential*.

National Instalment Savings

NIS pay 35 per cent interest after six years. Unlike Savings Certificates and Bonds, they do not require a lump-sum investment. You save an agreed amount (between £20 and £300) each month for a year, and leave the money untouched for another five years.

Miss one payment, and the maturity date is put back a month. Miss two, and the agreement is cancelled. Like Savings Bonds, NIS can be encashed after each full calendar year. They are also inflation proof and confidential. Here's how £100 a month (£1,200 after one year) grows:

Two Years	£1,254
Three Years	£1,308
Four Years	£1,386
Five Years	£1,488
Six Years	£1,620

NIS only guarantee a rate for six years, but you can lock in at another guaranteed rate, and switch the lump sum to another An Post product. This may suit parents who have less than 10 years to save for their child's special educational needs, and do not want to risk their capital in a unit-linked fund. See also Chapter 14, Children.

> NOTE: ACCBANK has an alternative to An Post's NIS. Always compare rival products before choosing one.

Savings Bonds

They pay 17 per cent interest over three years. You can cash them in early and get your capital back, plus interest, but must leave your money in for a full calendar year. They are bought in £100 units. Here's how a £1,000 investment grows after three years:

One Year	£1,040
Two Years	£1,095
Three Years	£1,170

The Compound Annual Return (CAR) on Savings Bonds is 5.37 per cent but some interest is paid as a "bonus" in year three. You will get no interest if you cash in your bonds within the first 12 months, and may lose some profit if you encash after that. Savings Bonds are index-linked. If inflation is higher than the guaranteed minimum, you will be paid the higher sum. The maximum investment is £60,000 and £120,000 for joint account holders.

Savings Certificates

These pay 34.5 per cent interest after five years and six months (5.54 per cent CAR). Interest is added at six-monthly intervals, which makes them a more flexible product than savings bonds. They are an excellent choice for lump-sum investors (max. £60,000 and £120,000) who want a tax-free, confidential return. You can also generate an income from them (see p. 230).

Prize Bonds

These pay no interest. Instead, your capital is guaranteed and you are entered for regular draws for cash prizes. They are a good place to stash away a lump sum for a year but inflation will soon eat into your capital.

Warning! An Post can take weeks to send back documentation for your investment. Keep receipts for all transactions. Bank and Building Society Accounts

---

Bank/Building Society Accounts

Demand Accounts

They give instant access to your cash, but pay very low yields — as little as 0.25 per cent in 1997 — and are usually taxed at 26 per cent. Only use them as a temporary home for money, as other deposit products pay far higher rates.

Fixed-Term Accounts

These lock up your cash for a specific term, typically between one month and several years. They pay a pre-agreed interest rate. Say you invest £2,000 in a two-year fixed-term account that pays 6 per cent gross per year. This yield will remain constant, even if interest rates rise. Fixed-term accounts are a good short-term home for a lump sum like an inheritance.

Guaranteed Interest Accounts

Fixed-term accounts by another name, these usually quote an interest rate for the full investment term — like 20 per cent over three years. If comparing returns with An Post's popular mid-term savings options, compare *net* yields, as bank/building society accounts are usually taxed at 26 or 15 per cent.

Notice Accounts

These pay better returns than demand accounts, but you must give prior warning — typically one month — before taking out your savings.

Regular Savings Accounts

Available at both banks and building societies, you must save a specific amount, usually each month, for an agreed period. You may get special incentives, such as a higher interest rate or prizes.

Special Savings Accounts (SSAs)

First launched in January 1993, these can be opened at banks, building societies and An Post. You pay 15 per cent tax on interest. Gross (pre-tax) rates on SSAs are very good, but investment conditions are strict:

- You must be aged 18 or over to open one.

- You can only have one SSA account, but married couples can open two single or two joint accounts.

- You can invest up to £50,000 (£100,000 for married couples).

- The account must be designated as an SSA, and the Revenue Commissioners can check the records.

- You and/or your spouse must be the beneficial owner. In other words, the account must belong to you, and not be opened on someone else's behalf.

- You cannot withdraw money within three months of opening the account. After that, you must give 30 days' "notice" for withdrawals.

- Bank and building societies can offer fixed-rate SSAs, but can only "fix" an interest rate for up to two years.

A lot of the products described earlier — notice and fixed-term accounts — are often available as SSAs. You pay less tax as a result.

Tracker Bonds

These were hugely popular in 1996. Tracker bonds are launched by banks, building societies and insurance companies.

Firstly, they (usually) guarantee your lump sum. They also "track" the performance of one or more stock markets during the investment period, typically 3–5 years. If the stock market index rises during that time, you make a profit. If it falls, you just get your money back unless the institution agreed to "lock in" any gains achieved early on, or pay a minimum "guaranteed" return. Some institutions also average out losses and gains in the last 12 or 6 months. So, if the stock market crashes the day before, you may still make some profit.

Here's an imaginary example:

The "Double" tracker bond is launched in March 1997. It is a four-year bond, and the minimum investment is £5,000. It will track two stock-market indices: the FTSE 100 (which reflects the performance of Britain's top 100 companies) and the US Dow Jones Index. You are promised 100 per cent of the "combined" growth in these markets.

The bond matures four years later, in March 2001. The FTSE has fallen by 12 per cent, but the Dow Jones is up 40 per cent. You make 50 per cent of the Dow's rise — a gain of 20 per cent. Your £1,000 profit is taxed at 26 per cent, reducing it to £740.

Some tracker bonds promise a tax-paid return; others deduct tax from any guaranteed return. They have some drawbacks; your money is usually locked up for the full investment term and the minimum lump sum is high — around £3,000–£5,000.

Credit Union

Credit union accounts are an excellent choice for single women, young families and older savers who plan to take out low-cost loans, but they are not savings accounts as such.

To borrow from the credit union, you must have a good savings and loan repayment record. When you first open the account, save regularly, even if it is only a small amount. Your savings are called "shares", and entitle you to credit union membership and access to credit (see also Chapter 4, Borrowing). Credit unions pay about 6 per cent interest, which is much higher than demand accounts. Interest (called dividends) is usually paid once a year on savings. DIRT is not deducted, and profits should be reported to the Revenue Commissioners in your annual income tax return.

Government Gilts

Gilts are IOUs which are sold by the government when it needs to raise money. They used to be issued on paper which was edged with gold — hence the name "gilt-edged securities". Today they are also called government stocks, or government bonds.

They are sold in £100 units as part of a gilt "issue". Gilts are usually snapped up by large institutions, like banks and insurance companies, which buy a large chunk of each issue. Because of this, they can be difficult to buy (or sell) in small quantities (even under £20,000), and one survey found that only 2 per cent of Irish households had invested directly in gilts.

Gilts have many advantages. They pay an income, usually twice-yearly, which is often fixed until the gilt reaches *redemption* (maturity) date. This income is paid gross of tax, so people with no taxable income, like students, can avoid tax totally. Gilts are "safe" investments, which guarantee your capital if you hold them to maturity. They can also pay a tax-free capital gain when they mature, depending on the price you purchased them at. As a 48 per cent taxpayer, you may be better off buying a gilt that pays low interest, but a fat, tax-free, capital gain.

Buying Gilts

Gilts are complex investments, riddled with jargon, but they suit some investors — especially older people who want a safe home for a lump sum. You can buy them through a stockbroking firm. Large firms usually set a high minimum investment, perhaps £20,000, so it's best to buy through a smaller firm. You will pay a commission charge ranging from £25 to £40, depending on the amount of stock you buy. Gilts can be difficult to buy in small quantities, but financial institutions have traded more actively in them since 1995 when they were permitted to become *market makers.*

NOTE: You can invest in gilts through a unit-linked fund marketed by a life assurance company, too. These funds spread your investment across a number of gilts, and you can also invest in a fund with bonds from Europe, or elsewhere. The minimum investment is smaller, typically £1,000 plus, and yields are paid tax-free. But you can lose part of your capital as fund managers "trade" in their portfolio.

Insurance Companies

Guaranteed Bonds

Similar to the fixed-term deposit accounts available at banks and building societies, these pay a pre-agreed interest rate over a set term, typically two years or more. There is a crucial difference. An insurance company may refuse to repay your cash early, or charge a large penalty, but returns are usually paid tax-free.

Bonds are tricky investments. Ask these questions before buying one:

- Is my capital fully guaranteed?
- Will tax be deducted?
- What will I get back for my lump sum when the bond matures?
- Can I get an income?
- What are the penalties for early encashment?

Tracker Bonds

Insurance companies (and stockbroking firms) also market these. Read the small print in the marketing brochure carefully, and never lock up cash you may need quickly.

SUMMARY POINTS

Prioritise. If you are a short-term saver, you want to keep your capital safe, readily available and earning a good return. You may also want a home for "rainy-day" cash, if an emergency strikes. You won't be too worried about inflation. Mid-term savers also need access to their cash, in an emergency, but they should think about inflation, and solid, low-tax returns. An Post is ideal for these savers. The investment you pick will also depend on whether you want to invest a lump sum or small sum — £10 upwards — on a regular basis.

Here's a summary of "best buys" for short- and medium-term savers. Long-term products are in Chapter 3.

SHORT TERM (0–3 YEARS)

✓ Good Option	? Be Wary	✗ Avoid
Credit Union*	Gilts	Demand Accounts
Notice Accounts	Guaranteed	Equities
Prize Bonds	Bonds	Property
Regular Savings Account	(Insurance	Unit-linked Funds
Savings Bonds*	companies)	Tracker Bonds
SSAs*		"With Profits" investments

* Recommended.

MID-TERM (3–10 YEARS)

✓ Good Option	? Be Wary	✗ Avoid
Credit Union	Equities	Demand Accounts
Guaranteed Interest Account	High-yielding Bonds	Offshore Insurance Funds
National Instalment Savings*	Gilts	
	Unit-linked Funds	
Savings Certificates*	"With Profits" investments	
Tracker Bonds*		

* Recommended.

CREATING A PORTFOLIO

This is largely a matter of analysing your needs, and spreading your available cash over a range of savings options. Here are two examples. These are imaginary people, but their dilemmas are quite real:

Case Study 1:
Single woman, high-earner, wants to save — but can't.

Maureen (27) earns £22,000 per annum and has just decided to buy a house by the time she reaches 30. She still hasn't managed to save a deposit, however, and is also worried about fees. She doesn't want her quality of life to drop too much, either.

Because she has few commitments, Maureen could save a large sum of money each month if she put her mind to it. It's not a good idea to start a unit-linked savings plan connected to the stock market (even a low-cost Personal Investment Plan (PIP) or Personal Equity Plan (PEP)), because of charges if she encashes the policy early. Maureen should probably start a Regular Savings Plan at a bank or building society — perhaps where she plans to take out a mortgage — and transfer this cash at the end of each year into a Special Savings Account (SSA). The regular savings plan will discipline her into saving each month, but pays low interest. Or, she could set up a monthly deduction from her salary into a high-yielding Post Office account.

If Maureen wants to buy a £50,000 flat, she'll need to find at least £5,000 for the deposit, plus another £5,000 in fees. She should also open a credit union account, as this will let her borrow cheap loans in the future.

Case Study 2:
Part-time worker, husband is made redundant.

Clare earns £15,000 from a part-time job. John has been offered a £30,000 redundancy payout. They are aged 46 and have three children. John has applied for other jobs, but they can only just get by on Clare's salary in the meantime.

This couple need good tax advice about the benefit of John investing some cash straight into a pension scheme, and other aspects of his redundancy deal. They should probably split the rest of his lump sum into several parts. They could use some to pay off small loans (credit card, personal loan etc.) to reduce their outgoings; invest in a 30-day "notice" (SSA) which pays interest as income; and leave £1,000-plus in a regular deposit account for easy access. Long-term investments are not a good idea, as their situation is still unclear. Again, a credit union account would give them access to a cheap loan if they need one later on. If John gets a job quickly, he might consider sinking a spare £3,000 to £5,000 in a tracker bond as a medium-risk investment.

To summarise, planning a portfolio is very tricky. It's vital to get good independent advice to make sure that your choices are well-informed and based on *your* needs.

CONCLUSION

Deciding how to save money is about personal choices. Try to analyse your needs and capacity to save. When your ideas are clearer, look for professional advice. Remember that a financial adviser may "push" a certain product, so spell out what *you* want.

Make sure you get "good advice", and consult several people if necessary. Never, ever give a financial adviser *carte blanche* with your cash. See Chapter 10, "How to Find *Good* Advice" p. 101.

Prepare questions before going for advice or a sales pitch. Keep a record of the conversation and all future correspondence in a safe place.

When you take out an investment, keep track of its performance. Make sure you get a regular statement, which shows how your deposit/fund is performing. Review your investment strategy regularly as your personal circumstances change.

4

Borrowing

"A credit card is a money tool, not *a supplement to money."*

Paula Nelson (1945–), US economist

Most of us have to borrow, but we don't realise what this money really costs. This chapter helps you to shop for different sorts of "credit", explaining what the alternatives are and where to find bargains. See "Options" list, p. 39, and "Which is Best" summary, p. 47. See Chapter 5, "Buying a Home" for mortgage finance.

THE COST OF CREDIT

To borrow cheaply, you must know the *real* cost of a credit deal. One yardstick is the Annual Percentage Rate. The APR is quite good, because it builds fees and the repayment schedule into a percentage. This example shows how a lower APR cuts your credit card bill:

Ann's credit card has an APR of 26.53 per cent. Running a £500 debt for one year will cost her £94.76 in interest. This assumes she uses the card on January 1 to buy £500 worth of goods, pays the minimum payment each month, and clears her bill on December 31.

If Ann switches to a credit card with a 20.33 per cent APR, the credit "cost" falls to £69.31. Both options are dear (compared to an overdraft) but the second card is cheaper.

Compare APRs when you shop for a mortgage or personal loan. Lenders must put the APR on their ads, but sometimes they quote a dramatic *flat* rate, too. This does not include loan-related fees. Compare the *cost per thousand* as well as the APR, when shopping for loans. This shows the monthly cost of borrowing each £1,000, and reveals the total cost.

> *Mary wants to borrow £3,000 over 4 years. The "cost per thousand" is £26. She multiplies £26 by 3, giving her a £78 monthly repayment. She multiplies this by 48 (months), making £3,744. The loan will cost her £744, unless interest rates rise.*

CONSUMER CREDIT ACT

The Consumer Credit Act 1995 set tough new standards for the advertising, sale and supply of credit (including mortgage finance). It:

- Gives you a 10-day "cooling-off" period to cancel a loan agreement. Housing loans are excluded, and you can sign a form waiving this right

- Forces the loan salesperson (or institution) to show the full cost of the money you are borrowing

- Requires the salesperson to be "authorised" by the institution they act for and/or the office of William Fagan, Director of Consumer Affairs.

This is just a sample of the new powers contained in the 75-page Act. Contact William Fagan's office (Tel: 01 402 5555) for details.

Now what are your options for borrowing?

OPTIONS

BANK/BUILDING SOCIETY

Dial-a-Loan

Several big lenders, including AIB and Bank of Ireland's "direct" banking services, sell loans by telephone. You ring up, do a phone interview and get a reply in about 24 hours. You usually need a full-time job, paying at least £12,000 pa, to qualify. These loans often have repayment insurance (at extra cost) and the choice of floating or fixed rates. Always check the "cost per £1,000".

Mortgage

This is a long-term loan, typically 20 or 25 years, taken out to buy a house. See Chapter 5.

Remortgage/Top-up Loan

Mortgages spread your loan repayments over a long period. You can also boost the size of your mortgage with a remortgage, or "top-up" loan.

Mortgage finance is 3 to 4 per cent cheaper than standard overdraft and personal loan rates and qualifies for tax relief, *provided* you tell the Revenue Commissioners and the money is used to extend/redecorate the house. But it can cost more than short-term credit. For example:

Clare is 5 years into a 20-year £45,000 mortgage (rate now 7.5 per cent) and wants a new bathroom: cost £5,000. She can: get a four-year £5,000 personal loan (11 per cent (APR 11.4 per cent)), or top up her mortgage to £50,000 and repay the extra £5,000 over 15 years. The personal loan is cheaper, in the long run, but can she afford £129 per month?

WHICH LOAN IS BEST?

Loan	£45,000 Mortgage Plus	
	Option a) *£5,000 personal loan*	*Option b)* *£5,000 "top-up mortgage"*
Rate	11% (APR 11.4%)	7.5% (APR 7.9%)
Monthly Repayments	£129	£46.20
Total Repayments*	£6,192	£8,316.00
Total Interest Bill	£1,192	£3,316.00

Tax relief not included
* Assumes no change in interest rates

Source: An associated bank.

If you have several debts — a mortgage, car loan, overdraft, etc. — you can repackage them into a single, low-interest loan. But if you have problems with this larger debt, your home could be at risk. Don't use remortgaging as a "quick-fix" solution for financial problems and never cancel an endowment mortgage policy to take out a larger one. This is called "churning"; you will lose money through early encashment costs, and charges on the new policy. Talk to a trusted financial advisor *and* your own bank or building society if you want to remortgage.

Overdraft

If you have a current account and a friendly bank manager, this is the simple way of raising cash. It is flexible, but expensive.

An overdraft facility lets you go into the "red" (in debt) up to an agreed ceiling on your current account. You can withdraw money by cash card, cheque etc., and only pay interest on what you borrow. The charges on unauthorised overdrafts are hefty. For example:

Jean has a £1,000 overdraft, but she takes out another £100 without permission. The authorised overdraft rate is 11 per cent, but she has to pay a 6 per cent "surcharge", bringing the rate on the extra £100 to 17 per cent. She also faces a referral fee (roughly £3.50) for each transaction that keeps her above the authorised limit, plus £5 for each cheque drawn on the account that "bounces".

WARNING: Overdraft customers also pay bank charges (see pp. 14–16). Because an overdraft runs for a year, you can also get too dependent on it.

Revolving Credit/Budget Accounts

These are offered by banks. With a revolving credit account, you pay a set amount into an account each month and can borrow a multiple of this amount. Budget accounts are current accounts that let you to dip into the red to pay large bills during the year. See also p. 12.

Term Loan

If you want to borrow over £1,000 and spread the cost over a few years, a term (or personal) loan could be a better choice. You borrow a set sum from the bank or building society, and repay it over a certain period — typically 1–5 years. Repayments are usually fixed on a monthly basis, and do not fall as you repay the loan. If you want the cash for home improvements, tell the lender. You should get a lower interest rate and may get tax relief on interest repayments. Compare the "cost per £1,000".

PLASTIC CREDIT

Charge Card

This is a handy, safe alternative to cash. Charge cards can be used in a wide selection of restaurants, petrol stations and stores. The two charge cards in Ireland — American Express and Diners — are prestigious, and have fringe benefits like insurance for recently purchased goods and free travel insurance if you use the card to pay for a flight/holiday.

Unlike credit cards, these do not have a *revolving credit* facility and you pay a big annual fee. But there is no pre-set spending limit, which makes them handy for business use.

Credit Card

Credit cards let you "roll over" a portion of your debt into the next bill, but the APR is about twice the standard overdraft rate — 24 per cent instead of 12 per cent.

The trick is to repay your bill in full each month — as half of cardholders do — or use the card for very short-term borrowing — at Christmas, for example. Most credit cards give you 25 days after issuing the statement to pay the bill. In theory, you can get a maximum of 56 days' free credit, depending on *when* you used the card to buy goods. You must pay at least £5 per month, or 5 per cent, whichever is the greater, and you accumulate interest on any unpaid sum.

Here's an example:

Yvonne O'Reilly buys £500 worth of goods on her credit card in the fortnight before Christmas. This brings her up to the credit limit on the card. She is normally billed at the beginning of each month, and gets her first post-Christmas bill on 2 January.

Yvonne's Credit-Card Borrowing

Date	Action	Interest Paid
December	*Spends £500 on the card*	*£0*
2 January	*Gets statement*	
25 January	*Pays £25 (min. balance)*	*£8.23*
1 February	*Gets statement*	
25 February	*Pays £475 (balance due)*	*£6.75**
Total Interest Bill		*£14.98*

* Interest charged at £0.27 per day, for 25 days.
Source: *Adapted from The Sunday Business Post.*

There are two main credit-card "families" — Visa and EuroCard. Access is the local brand name of EuroCard in Ireland. They offer similar benefits, and both can be used at 25,000 restaurants, shops and other outlets in Ireland. Visa and EuroCard are both accepted by over 12 million retailers worldwide. You can apply for a card at your bank or building society. University graduates, and other interest groups, can also get an *affinity card* which has a lower APR. You can also use your card to borrow cash, but there's a handling fee. Check out these fees in advance.

NOTE: Both AIB Bank and Bank of Ireland charge an annual fee (£10 and £8, respectively) on top of the government's yearly £15 charge. AIB Bank offers a no-fee option, but you have to pay your credit card bill within 10 days of the statement being issued. Gold cards have a high annual fee (typically £60+), but you get extra benefits.

WARNING: Unmarried women in their 30s without a mortgage are the most likely to get into credit card debt, and married people with mortgages are the least likely, *Consumer Choice* magazine states.

Debit Cards

Laser Card, Ireland's first debit card, was piloted in late 1995, and now used by over 200,000 people at most banks and building societies. It is more an "electronic cheque" than a credit card, as it deducts funds directly from your account when you shop.

Store Cards

The arrival of Debenhams, Marks & Spencer and Laura Ashley has broadened the choice of store cards. These cards are also offered by Brown Thomas, Arnotts, Clerys and Best (the men's clothing store) and are very popular with women.

They sometimes have a lower interest rate than credit cards, although the UK retailer's cards had dearer APRs in a 1996 *Sunday Business Post* survey. With the exception of the Brown Thomas Master Card, store cards cannot be used outside the chain that issues them.

You can use them like a credit card, to buy goods and spread the cost over several months. Terms vary, but you must pay about 5 per cent (£5 or £10 minimum, depending on the card) each month. The maximum interest-free period range is roughly 2 months.

These cards can be used to buy sale or "special offer" goods but are not good for expensive purchases, like fridges or washing machines, because of the high APR. It may be better to get a "zero interest" or cheap cash deal (see p. 47).

OTHER CREDIT SOURCES

Assigning a Life Policy

You can get cash from a life assurance savings policy by "assigning" it (writing it over) to a bank, or another party instead of encashing it. You can only assign "with profits" policies, because they have a guaranteed minimum value, unlike unit-linked ones.

Credit Union

The credit union is a source of cheap, flexible finance. The maximum APR is 12.68 per cent, on a par with overdraft and personal loan rates. But the rate is fixed, and cannot rise like floating-rate term loans.

Credit unions have other advantages:

- Interest is charged on a reducing balance, so the bill drops as you repay the loan

- Being a member disciplines you into regular saving

- You can get cheaper home insurance and VHI premiums through "group scheme" offers.

You can't walk in off the street and demand a loan. You must join a credit union: one in your area, or set up by your union, company etc. You must establish a track record by saving on a regular basis (weekly or monthly) before seeking a loan. Each credit union sets its own lending criteria. Some will test your repayment ability on a small loan, first. Each time you borrow, you will get a new loan repayment schedule. For example:

> *Janet borrows the £5,000 from the credit union over four years (48 months). She pays £104.17 per month, plus interest, but the interest bill shrinks as she pays off the loan. Janet pays £154.17 in the first month (including £50 interest) and just £105.21 in the 48th and final month. She pays even less interest if she pays off the loan faster than planned with extra monthly payments.*

When you borrow from the credit union, your savings stay intact. These "shares" are part of the credit union's communal pool of money that it uses for loans. You can withdraw money if you have no loan, and may be able to use some shares to pay off the loan — in certain circumstances. Shares earn a yearly interest "dividend", usually 6 per cent, which must be declared to the Revenue Commissioners in your annual tax return. Loans are automatically insured against death and total disability.

Hire Purchase

HP differs from leasing in that you own the goods you are paying for. The interest rates are often high, and VAT is charged at 21 per cent on purchases. As with lease contracts, there may be a heavy penalty if you want to repay early.

Car Purchase Plans

Most manufacturers offer finance packages based on the HP concept. These are cheap and growing in popularity. Instead of paying interest on the full cost of the new car, you pay interest on the difference between the purchase price and the car's minimum market value when the "plan" ends — typically three years. You then buy the car for that fixed projected value or start a new plan, with a new car.

Leasing

This is another way of "buying" a car or other expensive items. It can be cheaper than a standard car finance deal or a personal loan, because leasing companies enjoy tax advantages. Companies — including sole traders — can also claim tax benefits if they acquire a car through lease finance instead of through direct purchase.

Leasing is tricky. Agreements can include an extra monthly instalment as part of the payment schedule, bringing the total number of re-payments to 37 over 3 years, or 61 over 5 years. The finance company may also charge extra to release the car at the end of the term because the car still "belongs" to the leasing company, even when you are paying for it. These hidden costs can make it difficult to compare monthly charges, especially as leasing companies quote flat rates, instead of APRs. Ask about repayment costs per £1,000 borrowed, or the total re-payment cost instead. There can be a "deposit" charge, equivalent to several months' payments, and heavy penalties for cancelling a lease agreement or repaying it early. Always check the *real* cost of a lease deal.

Moneylenders

Even "authorised" moneylenders charge an exorbitant rate for loans. Borrowing from the credit union is a far better option. If you get into trouble with a moneylender, contact an advice agency, such as the St Vincent de Paul Society or Threshold (see Chapter 10).

Retail Credit Deals

"Zero-interest" credit and low-interest credit deals are commonly used to sell white and brown goods (fridges and TVs, etc.), and can be of benefit to cash-strapped buyers who have no other access to credit. Treat them with caution. If you can afford to pay cash instead, ask yourself: "Can I get this cheaper in another store?" Work out the total credit cost.

WHICH IS BEST?

✓ Good Option	? Be Wary	✗ Avoid
Budget Accounts	Assigning a Life Assurance Policy	Credit Cards (long-term borrowing)
Credit Cards (short-term borrowing)	Dial-a-loan	Moneylender
Credit Union	HP, Leasing	
Overdraft	Retail Credit Deals	
Term Loan	Remortgage	
Car Purchase Plans	Store Cards	

SHOPPING FOR A LOAN?

Five key questions

- Affordability?
- Alternatives?
- Cost?
- Flexibility?
- Small Print?

Affordability?

Ask yourself: Can I keep up repayments if interest rates rise? Should I choose a flexible option (the credit union) or a fixed interest rate?

Options?

Ask the salesperson: Can I take out a floating or fixed rate loan? What do they cost? Can I get loan protection insurance?

Cost?

What are the weekly/monthly repayments? What is the "cost per thousand"? What's the total cost of credit (if interest rates stay the same)? What's the cost if interest rates rise by 2 per cent? Are there other charges; insurance, final payments, etc.?

Flexibility?

Can I repay the loan early? Is there a penalty? Can I suspend or alter payments if my financial situation changes?

Small Print?

What happens if I can't pay?

If You are Refused Credit

You don't have a legal right to borrow money. If you've never had a loan before, a bank may reject your application, even if you have held an account there and run it properly. The lender may not have enough information to make a commercial decision about you. However, its easier to borrow from a lender that you have a "relationship" with.

The lender may turn down a loan if it consults the Irish Credit Rating Bureau. The ICRB has files with information on court judgements, tax debts, etc. You can access your file for just £5 and if the information is wrong, you can change it. Under the Data Protection Act, you can check computerised records held by financial institutions about you. If you have a problem, and cannot resolve it, go to the Ombudsman for the Credit Institutions (see Chapter 10, p. 107).

CONCLUSION

We all borrow money at some stage and many of us will carry a large debt (a mortgage) for 20 years or more. When shopping for credit, remember the following:

- Compare the "cost per £1,000"

- Don't overstretch yourself. Circumstances can change, often at short notice

- Consider a fixed-rate loan and insurance on your loan repayments

- Read the small print carefully

- Check out the credit union.

5

Buying a Home

"Everybody needs a home."

June Jordan, American poet, teacher (1936–)

Buying a house used to be something women did when they got married. Even then, the husband often paid the mortgage (house loan) and "owned" the property.

Not any more. At one leading bank, where 21 per cent of mortgages were taken out by single people in 1995/96, over half of these clients were women — 11 per cent, in total. Just two years earlier, single women accounted for 4 per cent of that bank's new mortgage business. Rival lenders agree: single women are just as likely as unmarried men to buy a home. Also, when couples buy together they often share the cost.

This chapter is about buying your home, on your own or with a partner. It includes a step-by-step "buyer's" guide, and helps you choose between the hundreds of mortgages on offer. It looks at pitfalls, too, like hidden costs and legal snags.

NOTE: If you plan to buy a house with a cohabiting partner, turn to p. 122 to check the legal and tax implications.

<small>The Buyer's Checklist:</small>

STEP 1: DO YOUR SUMS

Saving the Deposit

Banks and building societies usually lend up to 90 per cent of the house's purchase price. You must save the rest, unless you borrow (not a good idea) or sell one house to buy another.

Try to save regularly. Find a lender that pays high interest on your savings and has keen mortgage rates. Some give a special mortgage deal to their own savers, the so-called "qualifiers" rate. When picking an account, remember that Special Savings Accounts (SSAs) pay high interest and deduct tax at 15 per cent, instead of 26 per cent. You must leave the money in for three months, then give one month's notice before withdrawals. The Credit Union and Post Office are also good choices for regular savers (see pp. 27, 31).

How Much Can You Afford?

Apart from the 90 per cent rule, lenders usually limit the amount they lend to a multiple of your income. Typically, this is 2.5 times the size of the main applicant's gross (pre-tax) salary. Thus, to qualify for a £50,000 mortgage, a single woman would need a £20,000 pa salary.

Lenders sometimes take regular overtime and bonuses into account. If the mortgage application is in joint names, they usually factor in a smaller percentage of the second person's salary. Here's an example.

How Much Can They Borrow?

Based on a joint mortgage application by Jane and Jim:

Customer	Salary	Multiple of Salary	Borrowing Threshold
Jane	£21,000	2.5	£52,500
Jim	£18,500	1	£18,500
Joint Mortgage Limit			**£71,000**

Note: Limits vary from one lender to another.

Jane and Jim can borrow up to £71,000, but because of the 90 per cent rule the dearest house they can buy (unless they have savings) is about £79,000. They must find £8,000 for the deposit, and another £1,500 in costs. If they buy a second-hand property, or a new one over 125 square metres, stamp duty on a £79,000 house will cost £4,740. Their total shortfall is over £14,000 before decorating and other costs after they move in (see list, p. 57).

Borrow wisely. Many lenders give a cheaper mortgage rate if you want 80 per cent (or less) of the purchase price. Building societies charge an extra fee — the indemnity bond — if you borrow over 70–75 per cent. Also, remember that repayments will go up if interest rates rise, unless you choose a fixed-rate mortgage (see "Which Mortgage?" p. 62). Even so, the repayments may rise sharply when the fixed rate period ends, and you switch to a floating interest rate. Here's an example:

MONTHLY REPAYMENTS ON A £50,000 ANNUITY MORTGAGE*

Interest Rate	Monthly Payments
7 %	£393.50
8%	£424.39
10%	£489.42
12%	£557.83

* Gross of tax relief. Based on yearly reducing balance.

Source: Mortgage Advice Shop.

Each 0.5 per cent mortgage-rate rise adds about £16 to your monthly repayment bill. Mortgage repayments should not exceed a quarter of your net (after-tax) monthly income, as a rule. Use the budget planner below to work out your monthly income and outgoings. Leave spare cash for savings, and interest rate gains.

> WARNING: If the mortgage is based on two incomes, remember that one partner may lose their job or start working part-time if children arrive. Starting a family will also increase costs, unless you cut back elsewhere.

PERSONAL BUDGET PLANNER

Your Monthly Income

Salary (after tax and other deductions)	£..........
Guaranteed Overtime/Bonus (after tax etc.)	£..........
Payments/Commission	£..........
Income from Savings	£..........
Partner's Salary (after tax etc.)	£..........
Partner's Guaranteed Overtime/Bonus (after tax etc.)	£..........
Partner's Payments/Commission	£..........
Partner's Income from Savings	£..........
Total Monthly Income	**£..........**

Your Monthly Outgoings

Repayments on Personal Loans, Credit etc.	£..........
Repayments on Credit Cards	£..........
Regular Savings/Investments	£..........

Home Bills:

Electricity	£..........
Gas	£..........
Other Heating	£..........
Telephone	£..........
House Insurance	£..........
Water/Refuse/Rates/Service Charges	£..........

Other Costs:

Medical Health Insurance (VHI, BUPA)	£..........
TV (licence, rental, repayments)	£..........
Holiday Expenses	£..........
Entertainment Expenses	£..........
Sports/Hobbies/Clubs	£..........
Food, Household Items	£..........
Car (repayments/insurance/tax, etc.)	£..........
Fares to Work	£..........
Clothing	£..........
Miscellaneous	£..........
Total Monthly Costs	**£..........**

Maximum Monthly Mortgage Repayment

Monthly Income, Less Costs	£..........

Source: Adapted from AIB Bank's housebuyers' guide, "A Place of Your Own".

STEP 2: PICK THE RIGHT MORTGAGE

Get "Approval in Principle"

You've decided how much you need, and can afford to borrow. Now you have to arrange the loan. Many people do this by getting "approval in principle" for the sum they want. This is not a formal mortgage application, but an uncashable cheque that lets you shop for a house (in your price range) and pay a deposit in the knowledge that the lender should give you a mortgage in several weeks' time.

Pick the Right Mortgage...

See pp. 62 for the different mortgage options. It's vital to pick a mortgage that suits your needs.

... From the Right Lender

Most lenders can give "approval in principle" within 24 hours. Some do it through a mortgage broker; others may ask you to visit the branch for a personal interview. Many sorts of institution lend mortgage finance (see p. 61).

Shop around. Compare the Annual Percentage Rates (APR) on offer from rival lenders. The APR reveals the annual cost of servicing the loan, plus any fees related to the mortgage, but it's better to compare monthly repayment costs. If you get advice from a mortgage broker, ask him/her to quote for different lenders on that basis. Ask what fees each lender charges and how flexible it would be if you wanted to repay the mortgage early, or extend the term. Then choose.

STEP 3: FIND THE HOUSE

Do Initial Research

Get a feel for the housing market before arranging your mortgage to find out how much you need to borrow. Check out the property pages in the newspapers, and ring estate agents and auctioneers. Visit the area you plan to buy in for on-the-spot research.

Get Down to Business

Don't waste time looking at unsuitable properties. Contact several estate agents, giving them a clear idea of the type of house you want and how much you can afford. Ask yourself (and your partner):

- Do I/we want a new house (which is maintenance-free and may qualify for the £3,000 first-time buyers' grant), or an older house that has more character and investment value but potential problems (rising damp, woodworm, etc.)?

- How big a house/apartment do I need? Do I plan to start a family or have more children?

- Do I want to live near work, and/or family and friends, the sea, facilities such as shopping centres, a bank etc.?

- What sort of neighbourhood do I feel comfortable in? Do I want a socially mixed area, an upmarket estate or a settled area where property prices may rise sharply?

- Do I want a garden, especially one that is south-facing and not overlooked, a garage, a rear-entrance and a back yard for bicycles, tools etc.?

Do Your Homework

When you find a house you like, at a price you can afford, do more research before making a bid. Is the area "improving"? Are houses well cared for, and are values rising? Does the area have a low crime rate (ask the local Garda station or neighbours)? Are there development plans in train — like new housing estates, a road-widening scheme, etc. — that could affect your quality of life?

You may want to get the house valued and surveyed, now or later on (see p. 59).

STEP 4: DO MORE SUMS

Make sure you can afford this home. Houses have hidden costs and some, like stamp duty on old expensive properties, are punishing. They are often linked to the purchase price or house's value and can add 10 per cent to the purchase price. Here's a list:

Valuation Fee

The fee ranges from about £1.50 per £1,000 valued, to a flat £75-£100. VAT is charged at 21 per cent on top of this. The valuer may charge extra for travelling or other expenses.

Legal Fees

Charges vary. You must pay your own solicitor for the "conveyancing", or processing, of the transaction. The Incorporated Law Society suggests 1.5 per cent of the house's purchase price, plus £100 and VAT at 21 per cent on the total. If you are selling a house, you pay about 1 per cent, plus £100 and VAT. Bargain gracefully. Solicitors must state their fees, or guesstimate them, at the outset. Find out if the lender also charges for legal costs.

Stamp Duty

Buyers pay government stamp duty of up to 9 per cent on the "purchase deeds" of second-hand houses and new homes over 125 square metres in floor area (1,346 square feet). See charges below.

Acceptance Fee

Some banks and building societies still charge an "acceptance" or "arrangement" fee. It is linked to the size of the loan (typically 0.5 per cent) or is a flat fee (generally, £100–£150). Try to pay this fee "up front", instead of adding it to the loan and paying interest on it over 20 years! Better still, pick a lender who charges no fee.

Indemnity Bond

Building societies charge this if you borrow over 70 or 75 per cent of the property's value. The "bond" is an insurance policy that protects the lender if you cannot repay the mortgage.

STAMP DUTY CHARGES

Purchase Price	Percentage Charged
Under £5,000	0%
£5,001–£10,000	1%
£10,001–£15,000	2%
£15,001–£25,000	3%
£25,001–£50,000	4%
£50,001–£60,000	5%
£60,001–£150,000	6%
£150,001–£160,000	7%
£160,001–£170,000	8%
£170,001 or more	9%

Future Costs

Residential Property Tax (RPT) was scrapped with effect from April 1997, but it may be replaced by rates or another form of tax. Will you have to redecorate or refurbish the property? Also, a lender may insist on major work — like removing an illegal extension or installing a damp-proof course — before issuing the full loan cheque. You may have to pay for this, and the full purchase price, by taking out a "bridging loan" until the rest of the money is released. Hence the importance of a survey.

COSTS ON JANE & JIM'S £79,000 HOUSE (MORTGAGE: £71,000)

Surveyor	£100
Valuation	£125
Stamp duty	£4,260
Conveyancing + VAT	£1,410
Total Bill	£5,895

Note: If Jane & Jim are first-time buyers, they will get more tax relief on their interest repayments (see Chapter 21). If the house is new, they can apply for a £3,000 "first-time buyers'" grant.

STEP 5: COMPLETE THE TRANSACTION

This is the final, nerve-wracking stage of house-buying. Most houses are sold by private treaty. The process starts when you make an offer through the estate agent handling the sale, or directly to the seller.

Making the Offer

You don't have to match the asking price, especially if the property has been on the market for a while and the owners are keen to sell. If you are very interested, don't undercut too much. Your bid may be refused and weaken your negotiating position.

It is customary to make a token deposit, £100 or more, at this stage as a gesture of good faith. This is not the real deposit, which is usually 10 per cent of the agreed purchase price. Both payments are held by your solicitor until the transaction has been completed.

Offers should be made "subject to contract and loan approval". This means you agree to buy the house, *provided* it passes a valuer's inspection and you get the necessary finance. A valuer who spots serious faults may recommend a lower price or, in extreme cases, tell the lender it is unsuitable for purchase. Even if you have paid a deposit, you are not legally obliged to buy the property until contracts have been signed and exchanged.

Getting a Valuation

Some lenders will make you pick a valuer from their own "panel". Others let you to choose your own. An independent *structural survey* is also a good idea for older properties, and vital if you plan to buy at auction. It can cost up to £150, but should reveal serious problems like dry rot, subsidence and/or other structural defects.

The valuer submits a report to the bank or building society and sends you a copy. The lender then posts you a formal "letter of offer". This states the type of mortgage that you have chosen, the interest rate, if you have picked a fixed rate, the term (length of the loan). Thanks to the Consumer Credit Act 1995 it also shows the total cost of your mortgage repayments, and the impact of an interest rate hike on monthly repayments. Read this document carefully. When you have signed and returned it to the lender you have accepted the terms of the loan.

Conveyancing

Your solicitor now prepares the documents and legal searches necessary for your part of the transaction. This process is known as "conveyancing" and can take several weeks. The solicitor must check that the seller owns clear "title" to the property (is entitled to sell it) and must search for other legal problems. When this process is complete, contracts are exchanged and the solicitor gives you a "closing date" for the sale.

Both parties sign the documentation and the bank or building society releases your cheque to the seller. The solicitor wraps up the sale by arranging payment of stamp duty (if appropriate) and registering the title deeds in your name. The property is now yours.

Other Ways of Buying a House

Auction

This is far quicker. The property is usually advertised for a few weeks to let people view it. If you are keenly interested, get everything ready before the auction, including:

- a valuation

- other surveys and searches (on planning matters, for example)

- a cheque from the bank or building society.

Sellers usually set a minimum price called the "reserve", in case bidding is weak. Houses that are sold as part of a dead person's estate (executor sales) sometimes have no reserve.

Auctions are not for the hot-headed. It is easy to get carried away and bid too much. The sale is legally binding on the purchaser, so stay within your budget and note the property's faults. Houses sold at auction can have defects or irregularities — such as an illegal extension, or some other planning problem — that make them harder to sell by private treaty.

Sale by Tender

If several buyers match the seller's price, they may be asked to make secret bids in a sealed envelope in a "sudden death" purchase. The highest bidder with the finance gets the property.

WHICH LENDER?

You can get a mortgage from three main types of lender:

- Bank

- Building Society

- Local Authority

Banks and building societies offer similar products; fixed- and floating-rate products, endowment and annuity mortgages and all the extras described in "Which Mortgage?" (see p. 62). The interest rates are similar, too. Building societies are sometimes cheaper, but they charge an indemnity bond if you borrow 70 per cent-plus. Banks are also competing with cheap rates and special offers, like discounts and flexible repayment terms.

Remember:

- Compare the monthly repayment costs

- Find out what fees the institution charges

- Check the small print in the mortgage contract. Is there a hidden fee if you try to cancel or change a fixed-rate mortgage contract? Can you repay the loan early?

Local Authority Loans

If you earn under £14,000 per year, and have a mortgage application rejected by a bank *and* building society in writing, you can apply for a Local Authority annuity mortgage. If you have a partner, multiply the biggest salary by 2.5 and add on his/her income. If that totals under £35,000 you may still qualify. You must also have been in full-time employment for at least a year. The rate is 7.45 per cent (floating interest rate, including mortgage protection). For information, contact: Loans and Grants, Housing Department, Dublin Corporation (Tel: (01) 679 6111).

County councils and corporations also help local authority tenants to buy a home, be it the property they are renting or a private house. You can pick the floating rate, or a fixed rate of 10.7 per cent (full loan term). Contact your local authority or the Department of the Environment (01) 679 3377 for details.

WHICH MORTGAGE?

A *mortgage* is a long-term loan, usually taken out for 20 or 25 years with a bank or building society, to buy a property. The interest rate is lower than on a personal loan, because the house is used as *security* for the debt. If you cannot repay the mortgage, the lender can repossess your home to get its money back, but this only happens as a last resort (see p. 111).

A mortgage is tax-efficient because repayments on the interest you pay qualify for tax relief. The bank or building society charges you the full amount each month (gross of tax), but the Revenue Commissioners adjust your Tax Free Allowance cert (see p. 203) and boost your take-home pay to compensate. You must tell the tax authorities about the mortgage to get the relief, and can only claim for your main residence. Holiday homes do not qualify.

There are two main types of mortgage: the *annuity* and the *endowment*. You must also decide whether you want to *fix* mortgage repayments for a given number of years, or take a *floating* interest rate.

TIP: If you want to insure repayments in the event of sickness, redundancy or unemployment, add this to your "mortgage protection policy". These policies cost about £2.25 a month per £50 of benefit, so protecting a £200 monthly repayment would cost £9 a month. Shop around — you don't have to take the package offered by your lender.

Annuity Mortgage

Most buyers choose the traditional annuity mortgage. Each month, you pay interest on the loan and repay some of the borrowed capital. In the early years, interest accounts for the biggest chunk of these repayments; your mortgage will have shrunk little if you sell in the first five years. As the mortgage *matures* (gets closer to the final repayment date), monthly repayments bite deeper into the borrowed capital. Your tax relief also gets smaller.

Annuity loans are risk-free. Your repayments will pay off the loan, if you keep them up, but you have no chance of earning a tax-free lump sum.

Endowment Mortgage

An endowment mortgage is an investment hitched to your home loan. Monthly repayments are split in two. You pay interest on the loan for the full term, and a separate premium into an insurance-based endowment policy (either *unit-linked* or *"with profits"*). When the loan matures, the proceeds of the endowment policy should repay the sum you borrowed. If the investment does well, you *may* also get a tax-free lump sum. If not, you may have to boost repayments just to repay the loan. Most life companies review the performance of their endowment policies after five or ten years. They will tell you if there is any possibility of a shortfall and ask for a premium increase. If you want a review every year, write to the life company and insist on it.

Endowment mortgages written on a "with profits" investment policy are less risky than unit-linked ones, because the investment grows as bonuses are added to the policy each year (see p. 221).

Which is Best?

Endowment mortgages have advantages. If you sell your house to *trade up* to a bigger one, you can transfer the endowment policy — complete with any profit — to the new loan. The prospect of a tax-free lump sum is also enticing, given the huge cost of buying a house.

But they are risky. If you want to be sure the loan will be repaid, don't choose one. Never be pushed by an insurance representative who stands to earn a commission on the sale.

Fixed or Floating?

Picking a fixed or floating-rate mortgage also involves risk. With a fixed-rate mortgage, your repayments stay level for an agreed period — typically 1–5 years. If interest rates rise or fall during this time, your repayments stay constant. That protects you against rate increases, but stops you from benefiting if interest rates fall. *Consumer Choice* magazine warns that you face heavy penalties for breaking fixed rate contracts.

On a floating-rate mortgage, repayments fluctuate as interest rates rise and fall. It's best to pick a floating-rate mortgage when interest rates seem to be falling, and a fixed rate when they are on the rise.

Thanks to clever marketing there are now hundreds of mortgage options to choose from. Some, like the *capped-rate mortgage*, are quite useful. This is a hybrid version of the fixed-rate mortgage. It allows customers to benefit from falling interest rates but guarantees that rates will not rise above an agreed ceiling, or "cap". A *pension mortgage* resembles an endowment mortgage, but you pay premiums into a pension rather than a life assurance-based savings policy. Self-employed people can get better tax relief on a pension mortgage because of this, but a pension mortgage is no substitute for a good pension plan. It's vital to spread risk, especially if you are self-employed and relying on your own income.

Don't be swayed by gimmicks, as lenders can offer discount rates to attract custom. If a bank or building society gives a 2 per cent discount off its standard mortgage rate in year one, work out the savings on a calculator. Ask yourself: does this lender have a competitive floating rate? A mortgage is for 20 years, not one.

Comparative mortgage-rate tables appear in the finance pages of the national press. You can get similar information from a good independent broker.

TIP: If you are buying a new home, pick a builder who belongs to the "Homebond" scheme (run by the National House Building Guarantee Scheme). When you enter into an agreement with him, get an HB10 form to confirm this. "Homebond" guarantees you against: loss of your deposit or stage payments, water or smoke penetration of your home (first two years) and major structural defects (10 years). Ring 1850-306 300 for details.

EARLY REPAYMENT

You can cut the total interest bill on your mortgage by increasing monthly repayments or making a lump sum payment. This also makes sense if interest rates are low, and you are paying less than you can afford. Talk to your bank or building society.

CONCLUSION

Buying a house involves big decisions. Picking the right mortgage is just one of them. Remember:

- Do your homework. Work out what you can afford — and stick to your budget

- Get good advice

- Pick a mortgage you feel comfortable with.

6

Your Health

"Health is wealth."

Traditional saying

Healthcare — and how to pay for it — are big issues for women. As mothers, we take charge of our family's health. We also live longer than men, five years on average, but suffer from more chronic illness. A 1996 study by the European Institute of Women's Health confirmed this, but suggested ways to fight cancer, heart disease and osteoporosis (brittle bone disease) and other ailments. Prevention *can* cure, it said.

The row between BUPA, the VHI and Department of Health in early 1997 about "community rating" also put choice in healthcare cover firmly on the agenda. This chapter answers these questions:

PUBLIC HEALTH ACCESS

People *ordinarily* resident in Ireland are entitled to free accommodation and treatment in public hospitals, regardless of their income. You get free access to medical experts, but can't pick the consultant who attends you. This is subject to:

- a £20 per night hospital levy (£200 max. in one year)

- a £12 charge for "accident and emergency" admissions (if you have no GP referral note)

- the waiting list for the procedure you need — which can be months in some cases.

All women are entitled to a free "maternity and infant care" service, including the cost of GP visits during pregnancy and up to six weeks after the birth.

PRIVATE MEDICAL INSURANCE (PMI)

This can help you jump hospital queues and get better accommodation and choice. Instead of a public ward in a public hospital, it pays for a "private" or "semi-private" room in a public or private hospital (depending on the PMI plan). You can pick your own consultant at no extra cost, provided he/she has an agreement with the insurer.

Until November 1996, the Voluntary Health Insurance (VHI) was the only company offering full medical insurance to all Irish people. It lost its monopoly — due to EU law — and BUPA (Britain's largest PMI provider) entered the market. The row between BUPA and the authorities in January 1997 was about whether the UK company's Cash Plans break Irish law. The rules say PMI must be "community rated", which means you pay the same premium, regardless of your age, gender or medical history. So what do the VHI and BUPA offer, pending future changes?

VHI

The VHI has five different "healthcare plans", A–E. Starting with the cheapest plan, A, they pay for the following:

VHI HEALTHCARE PLANS

Plan	Hospital	Accommodation
A	Public Hospital	Semi-private Room
B	Public Hospital	Private Room
B	Private hospital*	Semi-private Room
C	Private Hospital*	Private Room
D	Blackrock Clinic and Mater Private	Semi-private room
E	Blackrock Clinic and Mater Private	Private room

* Excluding Blackrock Clinic & Mater Private Hospital. The VHI will cover 90% of the cost of major surgery — such as a heart operation — at both hospitals for Plan B & C members.

Source: VHI, Jan. 1997

As we went to press, the VHI paid full cover and accommodation costs, for your appropriate plan, in 87 hospitals (180 days a year, max.). In 16 independent hospitals, you are billed directly for an extra 3.5 per cent, adding £35 to a £1,000 hospital fee. This is called "balance billing". A few consultants who don't have agreements with the VHI may charge you separately.

Plan B is the VHI's most popular plan, favoured by 72 per cent of its 1.4 million customers. Also, 80 per cent of VHI clients get a 10 per cent "group" discount on premiums through their job, credit union, or trade union, etc. The table below compares the VHI's Plan B with BUPA's basic health care plan, "Essential".

Other VHI benefits include: payment for X-rays, laboratory tests, drugs, convalescence in a nursing home (up to two weeks, after a hospital stay). It reimburses you for a percentage of costs incurred outside hospital, like GP and consultants visits, through "out-patients" scheme. You must pay the first £250 yourself (£400 for a "family" claim) per subscription year. You can use a medical emergency service, VHI Assist, when travelling abroad (see p. 91). VHI does not pay routine dental, eye and ear treatment costs.

VHI Benefits for women

- £300 maternity benefit (after 12 months membership) for normal birth, plus contribution to epidural, etc.: £600 total

- For caesarean births, etc., full hospital benefits apply

- Home births (on application)

- £40 allowed (under "out-patients'" scheme) for pre- and post-natal doctor's visits in year of birth

- Babies added to plan at birth, but parents charged from that date

- Child rate applies to age 18

- No charge for 4th and subsequent children.

BUPA

"Essential", BUPA's core health plan, covers semi-private accommodation in over 70 public hospitals and a private room in about half of these. It is roughly equivalent to the VHI's Plan A and premiums do not rise with age. As with the VHI, you can join up to age 65 but must serve a waiting period if you have an existing ailment.

BUPA initially supplemented "Essential" with a choice of four different Cash Plans ("Protection 1–3" and "Gold") which you could use to upgrade your accommodation. They pay £30, £60, £90 and £150 in cash/kind per day, respectively, if you are hospitalised. Premium costs rise *sharply* with age, and the level of benefit chosen. BUPA has withdrawn these plans for new customers. It plans to issue new age-rated Cash Plans in 1997 and a more comprehensive PMI plan in addition to Essential. Existing Cash Plan holders will receive their benefits as promised.

VHI & BUPA Costs Compared (10% group discount included*)

Person	VHI Plan A	VHI Plan B	BUPA Essential
Child (0–18)	£55.73	£86.65	£50.04
Adult (19–64)	£166.58	£238.13	£155.04

*VHI plans and BUPA's "Essential" Plan qualify for tax relief at 26%, reducing cost by about a quarter.

Source: Institutions listed

BUPA's package is much cheaper than the VHI's plan B, and slightly cheaper than A. Because its Cash Plans are not community-rated older people will pay more for these, however. Essential also pays your total heart surgery bill at the Blackrock Clinic and Mater Private (not 90 per cent), and more generous payments than the VHI for cancer treatment, GP/consultant visits, etc., through the "out-patients" scheme. Like its rival, it does not pay for routine dental, eye and ear treatment.

BUPA Benefits for Women

- Special rates for cervical and breast cancer screening at the Well Woman centres and Bons Secours (Cork, Tralee)

- £15 per session for homeopathic & Chinese medicine (approved practitioners only)

- £300 maternity grant, plus extra fees (£600 total), after 12 months membership

- Home births, with medical approval (£300 grant in aid)

- Three out-patients consultants visits covered in year of birth (one with VHI) @ £40 each

- New-born babies added free of charge to policy until annual subscription due

- No charge for 4th and subsequent children

- Students in full-time education charged at "child" rate until age 21.

HOSPITAL CASH PLANS

Hospital Cash Plans (HCPs) pay a tax-free sum each day you spend in hospital, and are useful for "topping up" a cheap VHI or BUPA plan. HCPs sold by specialist non-profit making companies, like the Hospital Saturday Fund (Tel: (01) 874 2136) are flexible, and help pay dental, optical and alternative medicine costs, too. They also give a "maternity grant", and cover for children.

These HCPs cost from £1 to £5 a week, per adult (regardless of age), with premium dictating the level of benefit. HCPs sold as part of a critical illness policy only pay a daily benefit, usually after a minimum stay. Some companies offer age-related HCPs, but the cost rises sharply over age 50.

CRITICAL ILLNESS COVER

This pays a tax-free lump sum — typically £50,000 or more — if you get a serious illness covered by the insurer. The "menu" of illnesses always includes heart attack, cancer, kidney failure, stroke, but can cover other ailments, too. Look for a policy with permanent and total disability (PTD) cover and an HCP. Premium costs rise steeply with age and smokers pay more. Shop around for a good deal.

Critical illness policies pay cash benefits tax-free, regardless of claims made on the VHI/BUPA. Quite economical, they can help single people or families who depend on a single breadwinner. Remember that life assurance only pays out if you die. Why survive cancer and heart disease, only to face financial hardship? Critical illness policies do not pay for routine medical costs, and are not a substitute for PMI.

PERMANENT HEALTH INSURANCE (PHI)

If you become ill or disabled, and cannot work for a long period, these policies pay a percentage of your normal salary — typically two-thirds (minus any social welfare payments) — per month. Payouts are taxable, but you can claim tax relief on premiums (up to 10 per cent of your pre-tax salary).

PHI is dearer than life assurance or critical illness, even with the tax relief. Premiums are determined by age, gender and occupation. Thankfully, many company pension schemes include (free) PHI cover.

Check the small print before buying a policy. Some insurers insist that you are unable to take up any job, not just your own, before they pay out. Some may disbar injuries caused by dangerous hobbies. Insurers usually "defer" payments for a set period — 13, 26 or 52 weeks — meaning that you will have to depend on your savings, employer's generosity for that period. The longer the deferral period, the cheaper the premiums.

MORTGAGE PROTECTION

Most mortgage-holders have life assurance which will repay the loan if they die. It costs just a few pounds a month. People who take out new mortgages can also take out an accident, sickness and unemployment policy which pays your mortgage for up to 12 months. These policies cost more than standard mortgage protection and you may not be able to take out cover on an existing mortgage. Ask a good mortgage broker.

LOAN PROTECTION

Many lenders let you insure loan repayments against sickness, redundancy, death and other catastrophes. This insurance costs a few extra pounds, and is often worth the expense.

TOTAL CARE

Very popular in the UK, total care policies are a new concept in Ireland. They are taken out by elderly people to pay for nursing care if they become disabled or immobile because of sickness and/or old age.

MEDICAL CARD

If your income is below a certain level, you can apply to the local Health Board for a medical card. The income limits for receiving a medical card were as follows in January 1997:

- Married couple (under 66)   £127.00

- Allowance per child (under 16)   £15.50

- Single person (under 66, living alone)   £88.00

The income threshold rises if you are older, live alone, have other dependants, pay rent or mortgage, etc. You may still qualify for a medical card on "hardship" basis if you exceed these limits.

Medical card holders get free GP/consultant treatment, prescribed drugs and medicines, in- and out-patient hospital care, dental, eye and ear treatment, maternity and infant care (including an £8 maternity "grant"). Persons receiving certain Social Welfare payments automatically qualify for a medical card. Contact your local health board for details.

STATE PAYMENTS

Sickness

If you are a PAYE worker, and have made enough PRSI contributions, you are entitled to Disability (sickness) benefit from the Department of Social Welfare. The maximum rates are: £64.50 per week, £38.50 for an adult dependant (such as a non-working spouse/ partner who is not drawing social welfare) and £13.20 for each dependent child. The adult payments go up to £67.50 and £40 in June 1997. You must be out of work for at least a week to qualify, and need a certificate from your doctor. Your employer may pay your full salary, minus the social welfare benefit, for a set period.

If you suffer from an occupational (i.e. work-related) injury, you can claim Occupational Injury Benefit instead. It pays the same as sickness benefit, but you may get other support, including the "constant attendance allowance" or free medical costs. Contact the Department of Social Welfare (Tel: (01) 874 8444 for details).

Disability Allowance

It is a means-tested Social Welfare payment for people who are permanently disabled. The rates and planned increases are as per disability benefit. Contact the Department at (01) 874 8444 for details.

Dental/Optical/Aural Cover

If you pay PRSI at A or H rates, and have sufficient contributions, you may qualify for some free entitlements. Ring the Department of Social Welfare about this.

Drug Refund Scheme

This allows you to reclaim the cost of prescription drugs if they exceed £90 per three months. If you have a long-term illness and spend a lot on medication, you can get extra help. Ring your local Health Board for details.

NOTE: PAYE workers and self-employed people can claim a tax refund on any medical expenses not covered by an insurance policy, health board or other body. This includes the cost of long-term nursing home care. See p. 207 for details.

CONCLUSION

Protecting you and your family against sickness and disability is a key part of personal financial planning. Remember these key points:

- Health insurance is dear, but an important safety net if you don't qualify for a medical card

- Shop around for cheap, flexible insurance cover

- Spare a few extra pounds for loan and special mortgage protection

- Prevention is better than cure — both for your finances and health!

7

Protection

"Prepare for calamity not yet in bud."

Chinese proverb

How can you shield your family against serious illness, redundancy — or worse? "Protection" is a key part of financial planning, and you can buy basic insurance cover for a few pounds a month. Yet many of us don't do it.

This chapter covers four types of insurance protection, and some State payments. It also explains how to make a will — a vital piece of protection for parents of young children. "Your Health" is covered in Chapter 6.

"Case Studies", pp. 79–81, shows how three women solved their protection needs, with an insurance broker's help.

DO A PERSONAL AUDIT

Aim to take out ample cover for what you need, at the cheapest possible price. Complete this checklist first.

A) Do I have:

- A job? ☐
- A spouse/partner? ☐
- Children? ☐
- Other dependants? ☐
- A mortgage? ☐
- Other financial commitments? ☐
- Medical problems? ☐

Am I:

- Separated? ☐
- Divorced? ☐
- Widowed? ☐

B) Do I have:

- A pension plan? ☐
- Work-related cover? ☐
- Life assurance? ☐
- A mortgage protection policy? ☐
- Medical insurance?* ☐
- An income replacement plan (PHI)?* ☐
- Critical illness cover?* ☐
- Loan protection?* ☐

* See "Your Health", chapter 6.

Part A highlights *needs*. Add information like the size of your mortgage, salary, other financial commitments. Also, how many children do you have, or plan to have? Life assurance is a must if you have young children. Single people, relying on one salary to pay a mortgage, may need sickness and/or redundancy cover instead.

Part B reveals *existing* cover. Company pension schemes often include a death benefit (life assurance), and income protection if you fall seriously ill. Most new mortgages are covered by protection policies. Some old ones don't, or the policy might only pay out if the second mortgage holder also dies. Check this.

TIP: If you are separated, or divorced, talk to an expert. That also holds if you in a second relationships and have, or plan to have, children (see p. 14) or just have a "live-in" partner.

LIFE ASSURANCE

This pays a tax-free lump sum if you die. This can be paid to your spouse, partner, or any person with an "insurable interest" on your life — a business associate, for example. Or, it can be "assigned" (earmarked) to pay a specific bill, like a funeral or inheritance tax.

Irish people are woefully unprotected. Half of Irish families have no life assurance, and the average cover is £20,000 — barely enough to run a household for a year. The ideal scenario, insuring yourself for ten times your salary, may cost too much. If so, set a generous target and aim to increase it later.

If you have children, insure you *and* your partner's life with a joint policy — even if one person is a home-based parent. Replacing a home-maker with a cook, cleaner, nanny etc. costs about £312 a week, or £16,224 a year, *The Sunday Times* estimated in September 1996. Full-time Irish housewives spend up to 100 hours a week on household tasks, but value this work at just £180 a week — or £9,360 a year — according to Ark Life. In this 1995 Irish survey, four out of ten married women said they were "full time" housewives. Most (40 per cent of all married women) had no life cover. Yet women pay less for this insurance, because they usually live longer than men.

> TIP: Save money by picking the cheapest quote. If you are in a company pension scheme, check what cover it provides first.

You can choose from three different types of cover:

Term Assurance

The cheapest, this is taken out for a specific "term" or period, usually when your children are small. You get no money back if you outlive the term. Pick the "sum assured" (payout) you need, say £100,000, or a premium you can afford, like £10 a month. Premiums are fixed, unless you link them (and the "sum assured") to inflation, but the older you are the more it costs.

Convertible

This is a bit dearer, but more flexible. It also covers you for a fixed term, but you can lengthen the policy without fuss or medical examination — even if you get cancer after taking it out.

Whole of Life

The dearest, this pays out whenever you die. Avoid unit-linked whole-of-life plans that pay an investment-based profit instead of an agreed lump sum. The final payout may be small, so pick a "pure" protection policy instead. "Whole of life" policies are useful for retirement planning, however (see p. 183).

WHAT'S THE BILL?

Here's how three imaginary women solved their needs with an insurance broker's help:

Single Career Woman

Question: Anne (29) and Rob (33) earn £20,000 a year each. Both have income protection and basic life assurance through their pension schemes. She is moving in with Rob, and they plan to buy a house together. They may have children, but have no immediate plans to marry. What protection do they need?

Proposed solution: *They probably have enough disability and life cover at present. If Anne and Rob buy a house, they need mortgage protection on a "joint life, first death" basis covering life and critical illness as well. They might also nominate each other as beneficiary of the "death in service" payment of their respective company pension schemes. This should be done in a "Letter of Wishes" to the Trustees of each scheme. A "dual" critical illness policy, paying £50,000 if either gets a serious illness (plus £75 hospital cash benefit), would cost £35.33 a month.*

Young Married Parents, Both Working

Question: *Cathy and Jack (both 24) have a new baby and hope for a second. They are primary school teachers, earning £15,100 (increment scale four, Jan 1997) each. They are in an INTO-sponsored salary protection scheme but their life cover is just one year's salary per wage-earner. They want to boost this, and get a joint £50,000 critical illness plan, with £75 per day hospital cash benefit included.*

Proposed Solution: *Boosting cover on a "joint life, first life" basis to £100,000 (25-year term) would cost £17.25 a month. Or, they could get two separate convertible term policies with the same £100,000 cover; Cathy's would cost £10.32 a month, and Jack's £11.27. As a third option, they can get a joint term assurance policy (£100,00) and critical illness (£50,000) for just £31 a month.*

Farmer's Wife

Question: *Margaret (42) is married to David (48). They have three children, aged 15, 13 and 3. David's farming income is erratic, ranging up to £25,000, and they are heavily borrowed. Their term assurance is due to run out in three years' time and they have no other protection (apart from VHI cover). What should they do?*

Proposed Solution: *David should have life assurance cover on his loans. They also need a 20-year term assurance policy given the age of their youngest child, ideally £200,000 for David and half that for Margaret. David's policy would cost £123.60 a month, due to his age, but if he takes it out through a Section 235A "term assurance plan", tax relief would cut the price to £64 (relief @ 48 per cent). Margaret's policy costs £25.*

Because David is a farmer, he cannot insure his income against disability. They may be better off with modest critical illness cover and a savings plan (for emergencies).

Note: Pension and savings needs were omitted from these imaginary cases, for simplicity's sake. Advice and quotes were kindly supplied by LifeWise, a Dublin-based insurance brokerage that specialises in women's needs (January 1997).

ACCIDENT INSURANCE

This pays a lump sum if you lose an eye, limb or are otherwise disabled in an accident. Some policies also give a small amount of life cover. Accident insurance is cheap, and often sold in "mail shots" by financial institutions. If you can afford it — fine.

MOTOR INSURANCE

You can find real bargains here, because insurers view women drivers as a "low risk" category. A survey in late 1996, published in *The Sunday Business Post*, found a 35 per cent gap in the cost of comprehensive insurance (1992 1.1 litre Ford Fiesta) for both sexes. But the imaginary client — a 35-year-old woman — got quotes ranging from £257 to £390, so shop around.

What Does it Cover?

You can have three levels of benefit to choose from:

- Third party only

- Third party, fire and theft

- Comprehensive.

By law, you must have at least third-party cover. Cheapest by far, it pays up if you injure another person or their property. Neither you, nor your car, are protected, but you can claim on the other person's insurance if he/she was partly to blame for the accident. Third party, fire and theft pays if your vehicle is damaged by fire, and either stolen or damaged during an attempted robbery. Comprehensive cover lets you claim for any damage to the vehicle, including sly scrapes, but it's dear.

How to Pay Less

Use a good independent broker to shop around. Also, ring "direct" insurers, who sell insurance by telephone, such as Premier Direct, Celtic Direct (in Galway), Guardian Direct, First Call Direct and Quinn Direct. You can also:

- Increase the policy excess. This is the amount you pay, £50 or upwards, for repairs before the insurer chips in.

- Consider not making small claims. You may lose some of your no-claims bonus and end up paying higher premiums.

- Pass your driving test. Young drivers get further cuts if they do a course certified by the Irish Insurance Federation (Tel. (01) 676 1820).

- Get a vehicle with a smaller cc. Usually, the more powerful the car, the dearer the insurance.

- Fit an alarm. It will deter thieves, and you may get a discount.

- Do you belong to a credit union, professional body or a trade union? You may qualify for a group rate.

- Give up drink! Some companies give discounts to non-drinkers, but you need references.

- Drive carefully and maintain your car properly.

What's in the Small Print?

The cheapest policy may not be the best. Does your policy include:

- **An assistance Package?** Useful for women, this provides an emergency breakdown and repair service in Ireland and/or continental Europe. You may get free car hire and accommodation, too.

- **A No-Claims Bonus Protection or "Step-Back" Facility?** Some insurers protect your "no-claims" bonus against claims like theft. Others let you insure it at extra cost.

- **An "open drive" facility?** Do you need to drive other cars? If so, you may need this.

- **Windscreen Breakage?** This may cost extra, or be part of the comprehensive cover package.

If You are Refused Insurance

If you are refused insurance or get a very high quote, you can appeal to the "Declined Cases" committee. You must have written rejections from five insurance companies. Ring the Irish Insurance Federation, or the Department of Enterprise and Employment's insurance section, (Tel: (01) 661 4444). The Insurance Ombudsman's Scheme does not handle this type of dispute (see p. 109)

WARNING: All insurance contracts are based on "utmost good faith". If you fail to advise the insurer of a material fact — for example, that you suffer from an illness or have a drink-driving conviction — the insurer may dismiss your claim later as null and void.

HOUSEHOLD INSURANCE

More traps for the unwary here. Don't always pick the cheapest quote, as your house is a valuable asset, and worth protecting properly. Use a good broker, and look for a group discount rate.

Don't Underinsure/Overinsure Your House

Insure your home for the cost of rebuilding it — not its market value. If you underinsure the property or contents, the insurer may invoke the "average" clause. Say the rebuilding cost is £100,000, but you insure for £80,000. If you claim for a £50,000 repair bill, you may only get 80 per cent, or £40,000. The Society of Chartered Surveyors (Tel: (01) 676 5500) publishes a leaflet on rebuilding costs. On some policies, the value of the house rises each year; make sure you don't end up over-insured.

Contents Cover

It's easier to overinsure here. Some companies give an automatic level of cover; others charge a rate per thousand.

"All Risks" Cover

This protects items if they are lost or stolen outside the home. It gives useful cover for bicycles, jewellery, cameras and other items at a cheap price.

Discounts

A burglar alarm may reduce your premium, but ask if your claim might be disallowed if you don't switch it on.

Policy Excess

As with motor insurance, this exposes you to the first £50 or more of the claim. The excess for subsidence can be up to £1,000. Check that the policy excess figure is not too high.

STATE BENEFITS

Unemployment benefit/assistance

See "Social Welfare" in Appendix B, p. 252.

Rent and Mortgage Supplement

This is paid by the Health Board. You may qualify if you are in a financial emergency, and your family home is at risk. Ring the Health Board's freephone number 1-800-520520 for details.

Redundancy/Dismissal Payments

If you have worked over two years with the same employer for at least 18 hours a week (eight for part-time workers), you are entitled to payment if you are made redundant.

Your employer should give you a lump sum, but the amount depends on your age, salary and length of service. The company may give you extra but you must get a *statutory* minimum. If your company goes out of business and cannot pay, the Department of Enterprise and Employment will do so. You should get two weeks' notice before the redundancy is due to take effect. You can take "reasonable" time off during this period to look for other work. Your pay should not be docked.

The minimum (statutory) lump sum is not taxable, but you can be taxed on larger amounts. Contact your trade union and/or the "employment rights information unit" at the Department of Enterprise and Employment (Tel: (01) 661 4444). The Department of Social Welfare (Tel: (01) 874 8444) will explain your entitlement to unemployment benefit and other payments. Talk to an accountant about your tax obligations.

Don't squander your lump sum or entrust it to a fraudster. Look for sound, impartial advice. See Chapter 3, "Saving Safely", for investment options; see p.35 for a case study of a redundant worker. In a large-scale redundancy, the employer may hire a financial advisors to advise staff. Take up the offer, but make your own decisions.

MAKE A WILL

If you have young children, a husband, "live-in" partner (heterosexual or gay), or own a substantial asset — like a house — you should make a will. This is a legally binding document that states how your assets will be divided when you die.

If you die without a will (intestate), your property may go to people that you had not intended, see p. 234., and your children may not be catered for as you might have wished. You can use a will to appoint guardians for young children, and/or trustees who can look after a child with a mental or physical handicap (see also p. 138).

It costs about £50 to make a straightforward will, which is money well spent. Here's a simple guide:

Seven Steps

1. Make a list of your possessions and estimate their value.

2. Decide who you want to give them to.

3. Talk to a trusted solicitor about inheritance tax. It may be better to pass on some possessions as a "gift" when you are still alive.

4. Choose one or more executors, whom you also trust, to sort out your affairs.

5. Draw up your will with a solicitor.

6. If you opt for a home-made will — which is not advisable — keep it simple. Make sure it is also dated, signed and witnessed by two people.

7. Keep your will in a safe place, preferably a bank or solicitor's office. Review it regularly.

A *witness* does not have to read the will. Neither this person, nor their spouse, can be a *beneficiary*. The will is valid if they are named, but they will get nothing. An *executor* must ensure that your wishes are carried out, after you die, and arrange payment of outstanding debts (from your estate). Pick two executors, ideally, such as a trusted friend and family member — preferably all young, and in good health! If you are elderly or have no close family, ask your solicitor. Agree the cost in advance. A *trustee* is responsible for the running of trust funds, for example, if you leave assets to young children. A *guardian* takes legal responsibility for them until they reach 18.

All these tasks involve a lot responsibility, so pick the people very carefully and discuss the job with them.

When you die, the executor takes out a *grant of probate* to ensure that your assets are properly divided. They can hire a solicitor, or apply directly to the Probate Office, via the local circuit court (see also p. 233).

Your will is valid until you make a new one, or marry. You can also make a will in *anticipation* of marriage. Revise your will regularly. It should adapt to major changes in your life, such as having a new baby, breaking up with a partner, etc. Inheritance planning is a big task. Read the relevant sections in this book (see contents) and get good legal advice.

TIP: You can make a simple will for £40 (single person) or £60 (per couple) from "WillAid", which will donate your fee to charity. You must book your will by *February 24 1997*, as the offer is limited. Tel: 1850-214420. Complex wills may be dearer.

CONCLUSION

Protection is an often over-looked part of financial planning. Yet it buys peace of mind, at a low price. Remember:

- Identify your needs

- Shop around, and use a good insurance broker

- Don't always buy the cheapest policy

- Don't hide relevant information from the insurer

- If you have young children — make a will!

8

Travel

It's ironic, but even a holiday can be stressful. That's particularly true for working women, who often have to organise themselves — and the family — before a trip, and are worn out before it starts.

But planning is important, and can stop a stolen wallet or small accident from wrecking a holiday. This chapter is divided into three parts, each dealing with an aspect of travel. They cover these topics:

- Travellers' checklist   p. 88
- Working abroad   p. 93
- Summer jobs (students)   p. 94

TRAVELLER'S CHECKLIST

Don't forget money, insurance and whatever precautions you need to take for your health. A few contingency plans are also a good idea:

CHECKLIST

> ✓ Money
>
> ✓ Insurance
>
> ✓ Health cover
>
> ✓ Contingency plans
>
> ✓ Duty-paid?

Money

Take a mix of money if you plan more than a few days' stay. That means a credit card, travellers' cheques, and some of the local currency, if possible. Buy your cheques and currency in advance, and shop for a good rate (see Table, p. 91).

You usually have to pay commission — typically 1 per cent — when buying cash or cheques, but some banks and building societies waive this. Write down the cheque numbers on the piece of paper provided, and keep it in a safe place, separate from the cheques.

Bringing a credit card? Jot down your Personal Identification Number (PIN), and ask the bank or building society for a new one if necessary. That way, you can withdraw cash from foreign ATM machines but don't expect to find them on every street corner. You can also lodge money into your credit card account before leaving home, so you'll pay less interest on funds you withdraw.

WARNING: Use your credit card with care. Make sure a trader doesn't make two imprints of it when preparing a bill. Tell the card-issuer immediately if your card is lost or stolen, or you might have to pay a charge — about £50. You are not liable for fraudulent use of the card, if you have reported it as lost or stolen.

Insurance (for you)

Holiday insurance is a mandatory part of a "sun holiday" package — which is just as well. It's cheap, and can pay medical bills, fly you home in an emergency and pay for stolen items. Cover sold with the holiday can be minimal, however. If you need better cover, shop around.

Flights-only deals rarely include insurance. However, if you book with a credit card, you'll get some cover for nothing. Check with your credit card company.

Insurance (for your car)

If you bring your car, check if the insurance policy includes a breakdown and emergency service for your destination as well as the required cover. Pay a supplement, if necessary. Or, take out a "Five Star Vehicle Policy" from the Automobile Association — you don't have to join the AA to buy this.

A good policy should arrange for you, and the car, to be brought home in an emergency, and/or provide alternative transport. Check the small print.

A full Irish driving licence is accepted throughout the EU and US. If you're going somewhere exotic, take an international driving licence. It has enough languages to keep most officials happy. You can get one from the AA, price £4, if you bring your own licence and a passport-sized photo.

REMEMBER: Service the car before you go.

Medical Cover

You are entitled to free, reciprocal health care in any EU state if you have an up-to-date E111 form. Get one from your local health board, for everyone in your family, and have them stamped before leaving Ireland. If you are on medication, bring extra supplies with you and a prescription, if appropriate. Get any jabs you need.

VHI members should bring their VHI Assist Scheme card. It will cover you for medical attention appropriate to your VHI "class" when abroad. Your credit card or charge card company may also offer a medical emergency service outside Ireland. Check it out.

> TIP: You can travel on a tight budget by trading your house or apartment through the Intervac Ireland scheme. You pay a £55 registration fee to list your home in Intervac's directory — then wait for the calls from Florida, Paris, etc. Intervac is at (041) 30930, fax (041) 30929.

Buying Cash & Travellers' Cheques

Shopping for holiday money is confusing, especially when *Bureau de Change* tables are like this:

Currency	Buy Note	Sell Note	Buy Cheque	Sell Cheque
GBP	.9796	.9670	.9765	.9725
USD	1.6551	1.6360	1.6529	1.6470
FFR	8.9586	8.7421	8.8782	8.8275
ESP	223	216	219.97	218.65

Key: GBP = UK sterling; USD = US dollars; FFR= French francs;
ESP= Spanish pesetas.

Source: An associated bank (Jan. 1997)

Say you want to buy sterling notes. Ask how much stg£500 would cost to buy, and if this includes commission.

To do the sum yourself, divide stg£500 by the "sell note" rate (.9670) which makes £517.06. If commission is 1 per cent, add an £5.17, making £522. To convert sterling back to Irish pounds, divide the sum you want to sell by the "buy note" rate for sterling. Then add on the commission, if any.

When converting a sum in Irish pounds — say £100 — into another currency multiply that figure by the appropriate "sell note" or "sell cheque" rate. *Bureaux de Changes* often charge higher commission on small transactions; don't change small amounts.

TIP: When shopping for foreign notes/cheques, the higher the "sell rate", the less they will cost you. When switching back spare notes after the holiday, the lowest "buy rate" gives the best deal.

Contingency Plans

Be prepared in case a thief or accident strikes. Have these written down:

- Your passport number

- Travellers' cheques serial numbers, and where encashed

- The telephone number of your bank, credit card issuer, cheque issuer, etc.

- Your credit card number, flight reservation number etc.

- Your doctor's number.

For a few pounds a year, you can register your bank card numbers with Card Protection International or another company. If they are lost or stolen, CPI will reorder them and advance cash for a flight and emergency costs.

TIP: Did you know that you can bring back 45 litres of "duty-paid" beer, or 800 cigarettes from an EU country when you return to Ireland, in addition to "duty free" from the airport?

WORKING ABROAD

Planning a longer trip abroad, for work or study, is a bit more demanding. Have you thought about these points?

CHECKLIST

✓ A tax rebate?

✓ PRSI/pension

✓ Local tax system

✓ Your house

✓ Car

A Tax Rebate?

You can claim a rebate on Irish tax if you leave during the tax year, because your personal tax allowances are granted for 12 months, even if you stop work after six. You may be entitled to a second tax rebate when leaving your overseas job to return here!

PRSI/Pension Contributions

Working abroad can interrupt your PRSI "credits" record and jeopardise your entitlement to maternity pay, contributory pension, etc. But social insurance contributions paid in other EU States, can be added to your Irish record for pension purposes. This is also true in the US.

Ask the Department of Social Welfare (Tel: 01-874 8444) before you leave. If your employer transfers you, find out if you can contribute to the Irish company pension scheme while abroad.

Tax System in Your Host Country

If you are being posted abroad, will you be better off if your salary is paid in Ireland and some of it remitted to the country where you live? Ask your company accountant.

Your House

Leaving a family home for a year or more poses a serious question. Do you want to sell it, rent it out, leave it unoccupied or let a friend or relative live there? You may be liable to pay Capital Gains Tax (CGT) at 40 per cent if you sell the house when you are living abroad, as it is no longer your primary residence. Ask an accountant about this. If you let the house, you'll be liable for Irish income tax on rents, but you can dock mortgage interest payments, insurance and wear & tear (if approved by the Revenue Commissioners), agents' fees, etc., from any profit.

Car

You usually have to pay Vehicle Registration Tax when you import a car to Ireland — within 24 hours! VRT is based on the car's market value, which makes it expensive to import a vehicle. If you have been living abroad, and were the sole user and possessor of the car outside Ireland for at least six months before returning, you may be exempt from VRT. You must prove that all taxes have been paid on the car before bringing it home.

TIP: Working outside Ireland can affect your "residency" for tax purposes. Talk to an accountant about this. Also, the European Commission has produced booklets on living, working and studying in Europe. Ring 1800-553188 for copies.

SUMMER JOBS

About 30,000 students work abroad each year, many with the hope of earning cash for the Autumn term. USIT, the youth and student travel service (Tel: 01-677 8117), has a lot of information about summer work, including where to find it. Bear a few of these points in mind, too:

- ✓ Spending money
- ✓ Bureaucracy
- ✓ Social welfare rights
- ✓ Tax

Spending Money

Bring enough to tide you over. That means a month's rent, plus a deposit if you plan to rent a flat, plus extra spending money. You may have to wait a month for your first pay cheque.

Bureaucracy

Opening a foreign bank account can be difficult. Bring plenty of identification with you, including an original birth certificate, passport, letter from your new landlord/employer in the country where you're staying.

Social Welfare Rights

When living in another EU country, you are entitled to the same social security rights as nationals of that country. But you'll have to meet local criteria to qualify, so you might need an employment record in that country.

Britain is more flexible — and generous — than other EU countries, because of our historical relationship. Irish citizens were exempted from stricter controls on non-contributory State payments imposed in 1994. Don't expect to be embraced by the welfare State, wherever you go. Check your rights before you leave Ireland, and bring documentation with you: original copy of birth cert, your passport, letter from your Irish employer/college, etc.

WARNING: Don't forget your E11 form, which gives you public healthcare in EU countries. Take out insurance if travelling to the US, as medical costs can be horrific.

Tax

If you work in an EU country, the US, Canada, Australia, New Zealand (and others) you should be able to claim a refund of tax paid during a summer job. Talk to USIT and the Revenue Commissioners (Tel: 01-679 2777) about this before leaving home. You can claim the rebate after you return to Ireland, but remember to bring any addresses and paperwork that you need. Students working in the US on a J1 visa are exempt from US federal tax and, in some destinations, State taxes.

CONCLUSION

A little bit of planning pays off. Don't leave home without asking: Do I have enough:

- Money?

- Insurance?

- Preparations in case of emergency?

If you plan to work or live abroad for a long period, preparations can save a lot of money, too. Why spoil the pleasure of travel?

9

How to Save Time and Money

"The most popular labour-saving device is still money."

Phyllis George, (1949–) American sports commentator

Our lives are often far too hectic, as we juggle home, family and workplace duties. A 1996 survey of European women found that 33 per cent thought more "time" would improve their quality of life. Only 19 per cent wanted more money. Here are devices that economise on both.

TIME SAVERS

ATM machines

If you have a bank account you can withdraw or lodge cash, check your account balance, change your Personal Identity Number (PIN) at 900-plus cash dispensers in Ireland.

Bank by Telephone:

AIB Bank and Bank of Ireland have sophisticated 24-hour "direct banking" services that let you bank by phone. Why tear into your bank branch when you can dial a number, and:

- Pay the ESB, gas bill, etc.

- Order foreign currency

- Transfer cash between accounts

- and more, much, more?

Details: AIB (Tel. 1890-242424), Banking 365 (Tel. 1850-365365).

Bank by Computer

You can already shop on the Internet and will soon be able to do banking transactions by computer. "Shop Ireland", an Internet site launched by BoI, gives access to Irish retailers, but you can purchase from any provider who sells a service on the Net. Purchases are normally by credit card — beware the security risk!

Details: www.shopireland.com and Internet sites.

Book by Credit Card

It's quick and you should get come-back if you lose the tickets. You can book theatre, concerts, film seats etc. Ask if there's a booking fee first, and bring the card when you pick up the tickets.

Details: Phone book, news ads.

Catalogue Shopping

You can browse through in-store catalogues (at Argos, for example) or have one at home and buy through mail-order. A good way of buying clothes, if you hate shopping, but check the "money-back" guarantees.

Details: Argos stores, magazine ads.

Insurance by Telephone

In the UK, you can buy (low-cost) pensions by phone. Here, half a dozen insurers sell motor insurance "direct" and at least one, Celtic Direct, offers life assurance. Ring your broker, and they will shop around, too. Chances are, you'll save money.

Details: Ads, your broker, Irish Insurance Fed., (01) 676 1820.

LASER Card

Pioneered by Ireland's leading banks, this is a plastic card that works like an electronic cheque drawn on your current account. Bring it shopping, and the retailer will "swipe" it through the terminal to pay for your goods. You don't have to queue up at the ATM machine.

Details: Your bank or building society

MONEY SAVERS

Clipping Coupons

You can get special offers on retail goods by saving up "special offer" coupons and trading them in. It's a national pastime in America, believe it or not. Bulk-buying to get coupons has disadvantages — do you really want trays of pineapple chunks?

Interest-free Credit Deals

Common in electrical and department stores, they let you pay for goods over a period, with no interest fee. Check the real cost.

Loyalty Schemes

Supermarkets, petrol stations, bookstores — you name it, they all offer these. Many work on a stamp-per-goods-purchased basis. Each time you spend in the shop, you get a "credit" towards goods that you might buy in the future. Don't let loyalty blind you to higher prices.

Details: Store should have leaflets/cards explaining terms.

Frequent Flyer

An up-market version, offered by airlines. Each time you fly, you collect points which can be used to upgrade seats, purchase tickets, accommodation, etc. Advise travel agent when booking ticket, and present card at the airport check-in point

Details: Ask the airline you travel on most frequently.

Shrewd Management

Finally, here are fool-proof ways of saving money, but they take a bit of work:

• Start Saving	p. 26
• Open a Credit Union Account	p. 31
• Borrow More Cheaply	p. 37
• Sort Out Your Tax	p. 200
• Claim your Social Welfare Entitlements	p. 205
• Avoid Bank Charges	p. 14

10

How to Find **Good** *Advice and Help*

"A foole and his money is soone parted."

English proverb

Remember that old saying when you shop for financial advice. An alert, confident consumer is unlikely to fall prey to a fraudster. She is more likely to get "good" advice, too. In other words, a steer towards the products that suit *her* needs — not the salesman's pocket.

This chapter gives tips on finding advice and help, if you need it. It covers these issues:

WHO GIVES ADVICE?

Most people first get financial advice from a staffer in their bank or building society when they open an account or take out a mortgage. That person may be helpful and experienced, but probably not fully qualified to advise on tax, risk and other issues. They may also push products sold by their institution.

You can get independent advice from:

- Insurance brokers

- Investment advisors

- Accountants

- Solicitors and other professionals.

General insurance brokers give advice on non-life products, such as motor, house insurance; life brokers deal with pensions, investments and other "life" products. The Insurance Act (1989) says a

broker must have agencies (sales agreements) with at least five companies. A broker should suggest suitable, competitive products. They earn a commission from each sale but, ideally, will suggest non-commission products too and offer both fee- and commission-based advice.

An *agent* represents up to four companies, a *tied agent* just one. The tied agent sells just one company's products. They can give "good" advice, but not "best" advice.

Investment advisors (and consultants) sell non-insurance investments, like offshore funds, etc., but they can also be a broker, agent, or tied agent if they sell insurance products, too.

Solicitors, accountants and auctioneers also give financial advice, but tend to specialise in their given area; namely, law, tax and property. This makes them ideal for specific tasks. Some also have agencies with insurance companies, others with a building society that licences them to take deposits.

FINDING AN ADVISOR

The Golden Pages isn't the ideal place to look. Don't take referrals blindly from friends and relatives either. Take recommendations, but always check the quality of one advisor by visiting a second or third. Contact a professional body, like the Incorporated Law Society (01) 671 0711, Institute of Chartered Accountants in Ireland (01) 668 0400 or Irish Insurance Federation (01) 676 1820 if you need help.

When you find a financial advisor, ask probing questions, like:

1. Do you give independent advice?
2. Are you bonded?
3. Do you have professional indemnity (PI) cover?
4. Are you qualified?
5. Do you offer fee-based advice?

1. Do You Give Independent Advice?

If the person sells insurance, check their status. If they're a broker, do they belong to the Irish Brokers' Association or another body? Contact the Insurance Intermediaries' Compliance Bureau at the IIF, to see who they have agencies with (Tel (01) 676 1850).

2. Are You Bonded?

A "bond" is insurance that *should* protect you in the event of fraud. Its value is often limited, typically, the first £20,000 lost by all the person's clients. You need proof of any monies paid to your advisor, or to institutions suggested by him/her. Tied agents have no bond; their employer should make good any losses.

3. Do You Have Professional Indemnity (PI) Cover?

Another form of insurance, this protects money lost through negligence or mismanagement. Like a "bond", PI cover may be restricted to a certain products. Tied agents do not require it.

4. Are You Qualified?

Would you let an amateur fix your plumbing, or remove your appendix? People who manage your money should also be qualified.

Beware of someone who claims to be an "expert" in all fields. An accountant's strength is tax, not law. Large accountancy firms cover many areas — including inheritance planning, pensions and investments — but they can be expensive. Create your own panel of advisors. Don't trust all your business to one person.

5. Do You Offer Fee-based Advice?

Insurance commissions eat into your premiums, and affect the return on your investment in the early years. You may be better off paying an up-front fee.

An IBA member should answer "yes" to questions 1, 2 and 3, but *insist* on seeing their documentation, too. As a few high-profile cases have shown, dealing with an IBA member will not protect you against fraud especially if that person sells you a *non-insurance* investment, like an offshore fund. Good advisors should also quiz you. If you plan to invest a lot of money, they should ask:

- What's your attitude to risk?

- Do you want to keep your capital (lump sum) safe?

- Do you need an income?

- Should you use some of this cash to reduce your costs, instead?

A salesperson who doesn't listen, or who pushes a particular product, may be too interested in commission.

AVOIDING RIP-OFFS

Choose the advisor carefully, then do your homework. Decide what you want — security, an income, a risky but potentially lucrative investment, etc. — and make this clear to the advisor.

Take these precautions:

- Prepare questions before you meet the advisor or talk business on the phone

- Keep notes of the advice you get

- Ask the advisor to state his/her terms, conditions, fees and advice, in writing

- Read all policy documents. With insurance products, you have a 15-day "cooling off period" to cancel a signed agreement. Check for hidden penalties and clauses in loan agreements

- With investments, make out the cheque to the insurer, bank, etc. Cross it and get a receipt from the advisor. Better still, pay in the money yourself.

- If you suspect trouble, get help quickly (see below).

THE LAW

Irish legislation is more piecemeal than Britain's all-embracing Financial Service Act, 1986. The UK Act created a powerful watchdog, SIB, which monitors self-regulatory bodies and the groups which represent lawyers, accountants, etc. The UK's Personal Investment Authority (PIA) deals with investor complaints, and pays compensation.

In Ireland, the State has opted for a large degree of "self-regulation". Banks, building societies and insurance companies have representative bodies. These organisations have "Codes of Conduct" to police their members, but do not fine or publicly reprimand them — as SIB does — for breaches in standards.

Supervisory duties are split between the Central Bank, the Director of Consumer Affairs and government departments. Each body "polices" a number of laws — over 100 in the case of the Director of Consumer Affairs. Some legislation, such as the Consumer Credit Act, is policed by two bodies each with statutory powers (freedom to prosecute). The key laws include:

- Sale of Goods & Supply of Services Act (1980)

- Building Societies Act (1989)

- Insurance Act (1989)

- Pensions Act (1990)

- Consumer Credit Act (1995)

- Investment Intermediaries Act (1995)

NOTE: The Investment Intermediaries Act, which monitors the sale of non-insurance investment products will be redrafted in 1997. This law now being policed by the Central Bank, requires people who offer investment advice to be registered, bonded and keep proper accounts and records. Compensation funds are also being planned for insurance and non-insurance investments. At present, you are only covered if you are sold a product by:

- an IBA broker (insurance product only);

- a tied agent, or

- a solicitor, estate agent, accountant with a bond or PI cover.

CONSUMER AIDS

What if you get "bad" advice, or are unhappy for another reason? First, raise the problem with the person who sold you the product or service, unless you suspect that person of fraud. If so, consult a solicitor and/or the police.

Next, contact the customer services department of his/her company — if appropriate. Write a short, courteous letter that outlines the problem clearly and states how you would like it resolved, for example, repayment of premiums with interest, if you were sold the "wrong" insurance policy. Give the company time to respond, but set a deadline.

Finally, you can bring your case, free of charge, to one of the Ombudsman's schemes. Your case must fall within the scheme's remit. You also need a "sign off" letter from the insurance company, bank or building society.

Here's where to go if you have a problem:

WHERE DO I COMPLAIN?

Banks & Building Societies	Ombudsman for the Credit Institutions* 8 Adelaide Court, Adelaide Road, Dublin 2. Tel: (01) 478 3755
Data protection	Data Protection Commissioner Block 4, Irish Life Centre, Talbot Street, Dublin 1. Tel. (01) 874 8544
Goods & Services	Director of Consumer Affairs** Tel: (01) 402 5500 Tel: (021) 274099
Insurance: **Broker**	Irish Brokers' Association 87, Merrion Square, Dublin 2. Tel: (01) 661 3067
Tied agent	The insurance company
Other	Insurance Information Service*** Irish Insurance Federation, 39, Molesworth Street, Dublin 2. Tel: (01) 676 1914 Dept. of Enterprise & Employment Kildare Street, Dublin 2. Tel: (01) 661 4444 Insurance Ombudsman 77, Merrion Square, Dublin 2. Tel: (01) 662 0899

*   This Ombudsman takes cases on behalf of small companies, and members of the public.

**   Runs a Consumer information "helpline". The DCA will set up another office in 1997 to deal with cross-EU consumer disputes.

***   If you are refused insurance, or get an excessive quote.

Other Options:

The Small Claims Court

This handles disputes between consumers and retailers and/or people who have provided a service of a non-financial nature. The procedure is simple, and administered by the District Courts. It costs £5, excluding the cost of witnesses, etc. You can only bring a case if the amount at dispute is under £600. Contact your district court or:

> The Department of Justice
> 72 St Stephen's Green, Dublin 2
> Tel: (01) 678 9711.

The Consumers' Association of Ireland

CAI offers a "Consumer Personal Service" for a fixed payment of £19 (£16 for CAI members). You will only be charged if CAI takes on your case. You can contact the service at:

> Consumers' Association of Ireland
> 45 Upper Mount Street,
> Dublin 2. Tel. (01) 661 2293

Irish Insurance Federation

The IIF has tackled several consumer issues. Recent measures include: new minimum training standards for all insurance sales representatives, a register of their employment histories to help root out "cowboy" reps., safety campaigns and "young driver" initiatives to cut motor premiums, and information leaflets such as *Life Assurance: A Buyer's Guide*. See table on p. 108 for address.

HELP WITH DEBT

It's easy to get into debt, especially if you have a credit card and a taste for clothes! But even small debt is a nagging worry, especially if you have an overdraft, car loan or other borrowings on top of a mortgage. Losing your job through sickness, redundancy etc., or the break-up of your relationship or marriage, can pitch you into a serious situation. It may even result in the loss of your car (if it is leased), or home. You can tackle debt with a series of steps, but note that small debts are easier to sort out than bigger ones. Keep an emergency nest egg, and don't let money problems get out of hand.

Step Number One

Fill in the budget planner shown at the start of the book (see p. 7). Work out:

- How much you are spending each month

- Where you can economise

- Ways to generate more cash.

If you are in debt with a credit card company, building society, etc., be up-front. Don't ignore warning letters. You increase your options, such as reducing repayments for a negotiated period, if you alert the lender at an early stage.

Step Number Two

Get advice. Some lenders offer an in-house counselling service, but you can also get independent help from:

Threshold

A voluntary agency, Threshold can give free advice on house-related debts (arising from overdue rent, mortgage repayments, etc.) and may help negotiate with the lender. It offers an excellent service. Contact:

Head Office,
Church Street,
Dublin 7. Tel. (01) 872 6311

8 Fr Mathew Quay,
Cork. Tel. (021) 271250

Augustine House,
St. Augustine Street,
Galway. Tel. (091) 563080

FISC

The Leinster Society of Chartered Accountants runs a free information service for people who need help with tax, budgeting, debt. etc. It is called the Financial Information Services Centre (FISC), and is held at "clinics" across Ireland. Contact FISC at (01) 668 2044.

Money Advice Centres

The MABs offer an excellent debt counselling service at centres around Ireland. They are funded by the Department of Social Welfare, and help both low- and middle-income clients free of charge. They can also try to negotiate with creditors and help you claim your full Social Welfare entitlements. Contact your local Social Welfare office.

Step Number Three

Find out what you owe, and the cheapest way of repaying it. A credit card debt costs over 20 per cent a year to "service", while an overdraft (not an ideal alternative) costs only 11 per cent.

Here's a possible remedy for a small debt (under £2,000):

- Take out a flexible credit union loan (that you can afford)

- Repay the old debt/s

- Remove the temptation — cancel your credit card, store card or overdraft facility

MORTGAGE ARREARS

This is a very serious problem, but the steps outlined above can also help. The flow chart on the next page shows what can happen if you do not reach an early settlement with your bank or building society:

How the Problems of Mortgage Arrears Can Escalate

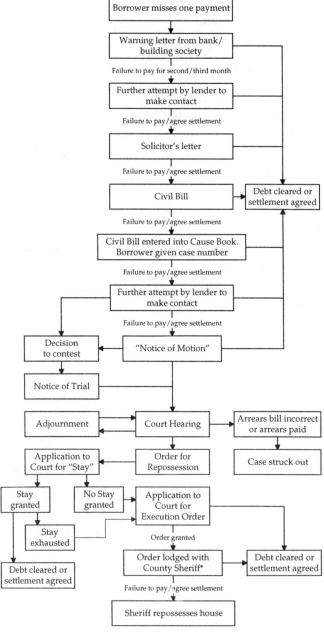

* Dublin and Cork have city and county sheriffs. The rest of the country has registrars who perform the same function.

Appearing in Court

If you fall behind with repayments, and do not meet the lender's demands, you will probably receive a Civil Bill. This states that proceedings are about to start in the Circuit Court (or High Court). You have 14 days to reply to this document, and it you don't, the civil bill is entered in the Cause Book. You will then be issued a number; for example, No. 3,000 of 1997.

Very often, mortgage arrears cases involve many visits to court (each adding to the bill's cost) over a two-year period, or longer. The judge has three options on each court appearance:

- Adjourn the case

- Strike out the case (if the arrears bill is incorrect, for example, or arrears have been repaid)

- Make an Order for Repossession.

Even if the judge takes the last course of action — for example, after ordering several adjournments — you can still save your home. You can ask the judge for a "Stay", to buy time if you hope to resume payments. When the Stay has been exhausted, or if no Stay has been granted, the lender's solicitor can apply to the court office for an Execution Order. When the court office has issued the Order, it can be lodged with the Sheriff or County Registrar.

You can still try to reach a settlement at this late stage. If you fail, the Sheriff can then repossess the house.

Solving the Problem

Banks and building societies respond far better if you contact them before your debt is huge. They may:

- Reschedule the mortgage. Your monthly repayments will fall if the debt is spread over a longer term. The lender is more likely to agree if the mortgage has a few years left to run.

- Let you pay interest only. This is very rare, but your lender may do it for a limited period if you promise to resume full payments soon. Or, your lender may accept interest-only payments from your local Health Board (see below).

- Get help from another party, such as a friend or house-holder, to pay the mortgage. This might create legal complications, however.

Your lender is more likely to seek a repossession order if you have built up a large debt.

How to Boost your Income

- Take in a lodger

- Ask the local Health Board or community welfare officer for a mortgage supplement. The Health Board may do this, especially if you have children and can prove genuine hardship. The payment is means-tested (Freephone 1-800-520520).

- Claim other social welfare benefits (see p. 205).

- Claim extra tax reliefs and allowances.

- Try the Society of St Vincent de Paul or other agencies for emergency help (Tel: (01) 838 4164).

The number of mortgage arrears cases rose sharply after the 1992 "currency crisis", then fell dramatically. Interest rates are low, but if you overstretch yourself by borrowing too much you could face problems later. Borrow wisely, and remember to save.

CONCLUSION

Stand up for your rights! A well-informed, confident consumer has far less risk of being ripped off. But if you do get into trouble, look for help, quickly.

Part 2

Life-Cycle Planning

11

Single

"A woman's life can really be a succession of lives ..."

Wallis, Duchess of Windsor (1896–1986)

Financial planning must adapt to "life cycle" changes, like getting married, having a child, breaking up with a partner or losing them — to serious illness, or death. Your needs and priorities will change with life itself. This is especially true of women.

Ask any mother how much her life changed when her first baby arrived!

This section of the book covers "life cycle" planning, and helps you deal with and anticipate some of these changes. It is divided into six chapters, each covering a distinct phase that may occur in a lifetime, such as marriage, parenthood and separation. Chapter 24, "Widowhood", p. 242, deals with the loss of a partner. The table, shown overleaf, maps the broad changes in a woman's life and how she can cater for them, but it is very general. Few lives fit into such neat boxes!

The rest of the chapter covers financial planning for single people. The first section, "banking", is chiefly aimed at students. If you are working, and want a wider choice of accounts, see "Starting to Plan" p. 6. Advice on savings, pensions, protection and tax is for all working single women. Single parents, see Chapter 14, "Children", and Chapter 17 "Flexi-work".

LIFE-CYCLE PLANNING

Age	Status	Financial Priorities	Solutions
Early 20s	Earning Independent	Personal Spending Mortgage	Savings/Loans Mortgages Personal Pension
Late 20s/ Early 30s	Relationships, Marriage/Cohabitation Young Family — tight budget	Children Household Mortgage	Savings (An Post, etc.) Term Assurance Other family protection plans
30s	Children growing up Women returning to work Some couples separated/divorced	Mortgage Pension interest starts	Pensions Savings for school fees (An Post or insurance-based)
40–50	More mothers in full-time work Teenagers at home	Pensions Investment of lump-sum inheritance Top-up pension	AVCs*, Lump-sum Investments
60+	Retired/Widowed Children left home	Enough money for old age Safe investments for leaving to children	Annuities Income-generating Investments Inheritance Tax Planning

* AVC = Additional Voluntary Contributions.

Banking

When you start college, you'll probably open a bank or building society account to lodge your grant, pay bills, and get cash from ATM machines. Banks want your business, and offer incentives like cash/gift vouchers, low-cost loans, etc. So shop around.

Run the account well, and your bank manager might be more sympathetic if cash gets tight. Don't abuse your cheque book, if you get one. The charges are also steep. Ask the bank for a short-term overdraft, but be prepared for a refusal. Most banks offer student loans, but they might ask your parents, or another person, to act as "guarantor".

If you don't need a chequebook, try a building society savings account. You still get an ATM card and interest (small) on your savings. Building societies don't give overdrafts, under any circumstances. See "Starting to Plan", p. 6, for options.

Savings and Loans

When you start working, you'll have more money to spend and save. You can apply for a credit card, and also borrow more easily. Work on a savings habit, too. If you open a credit union account, you can borrow flexible loans for holidays or your first car, later on. A building society or bank is a good place to save up a deposit for your house. If you're not disciplined enough to save, set up a monthly direct debit from your current account.

Pension

By your late 20s, it's time to start saving for a pension — see p. 185 if you need convincing! If you are a 48 per cent taxpayer, a £40 monthly pension contribution costs barely £20, after tax and PRSI relief. It's easier to save when you are single and have fewer commitments. Also, the longer you save, the more you accumulate.

You are unlikely to save too much (the maximum you can take is two thirds of your salary on retirement), given the probability of career breaks, etc. By your 30s and 40s, pay in what you can comfortably afford, but don't ignore short-term savings.

Protection

Consider these options:

- Critical illness   p. 71

- Health insurance   p. 66

- Mortgage protection (including critical illness
  and redundancy cover)   p. 72

- Permanent Health Insurance   p. 72

Your main worry is making sure the mortgage, rent and other bills are paid if you get ill, or lose your job. Single women don't need life assurance, unless they have children or support other people. Don't waste your money.

Tax

Single people are treated as separate entities by the Revenue Commissioners, and get the *allowances* shown below. Boost your pay by claiming all the allowances and *reliefs* you can (see p. 205).

ALLOWANCES

	1996/97	1997/98
Single Person	£2,650	£2,900
One Parent family* (single parent/deserted/separated)	£2,650	£2,900
PAYE Allowance[†]	£800	£800
PRSI Allowance[†]	£140	scrapped
Age Allowance[‡]	£200	£400

* Single parents get a £5,800 allowance (£2,900 single person & £2,900 lone parents), if they have at least one dependent child. This is the same as a married person's allowance, but they do not qualify for double tax bands. Widowed people also get special allowances.

† This can only be claimed if you are in PAYE employment.

‡ For people aged 65+.

Note: You may qualify for other reliefs if you have an incapacitated child, or another dependant. Ask your local tax office. For mortgage relief, rent relief and others, see Allowances table on p. 205 of Chapter 21.

12

Cohabitation

"Love one another, but make not a bond of love."

Kahlil Gibran (1833-1931), Lebanese mystic

You don't *have* to marry to love a person or have children. Some women prefer the informality of a "live-in" relationship. Others can't marry, because their partner is unwilling, a separated man or another woman. Many of these couples opt for cohabitation.

Unfortunately, people who cohabit are *strangers in law* in terms of tax and inheritance rights. A "common-law" wife — even of 20 year's standing — has very few rights, but you can use financial planning to create closer ties, if you wish. This chapter covers these topics:

• Banking	p. 121
• Savings	p. 121
• Pensions	p. 121
• Protection	p. 122
• Tax	p. 122
• Property	p. 122
• Social welfare	p. 123

Banking

You may want to open a *joint account* with your partner to simplify the payment of rent, bills, etc. If you ask for *sole* authorisation on the account, the bank will let either of you sign cheques. *Joint* authorisation, where both have to sign, is more common in business relationships.

You have to trust your partner totally if you choose sole authorisation, as either of you could strip the account bare. Two separate current accounts might be simpler, and would give you more independence.

Legally, anything held in "joint names" is 50 per cent owned by both parties. That applies to bank balances and overdrafts. If either partner dies, their share of the joint asset goes to the other person, broadly speaking (see p. 244). So will any debts.

Savings

When you move in with a partner, you probably won't think about joint savings or investment accounts, unless you plan to buy a home together. You can open accounts in joint names, but sometimes the first-named person on the account has more rights — for example, in the event of a "free share" allowance being handed out. Talk to An Post about your options, too.

Pension

Cohabitation affects pension planning. You are not entitled to a spouses' pension from Social Welfare, for example, even if you have a family. Your children should be entitled to a dependant's pension, however.

Members of company pension schemes can nominate their partner for the *death-in-service benefit*. This lump sum, usually a multiple of salary, is paid if you die while employed by the company. To request this, send a "Letter of Wishes" to the scheme's trustees. They can ignore your request, but may equally decide to give your partner part of a spouse's pension — if one exists in the scheme. That depends on the scheme rules, and on the trustees. The surviving partner may have to request this payment, and support the claim with documents that prove financial inter-dependence, such as gas bills, mortgage statements, etc. Bear in mind that your partner's family *may* resist your claim.

Protection

Life companies will provide a life assurance policy if you can prove an *insurable interest* in the other person's life. A couple living together, especially with children, should qualify. Term assurance on a "joint-life" basis is relatively cheap, and pays a specified sum if either of the two insured "names" dies within a specific period. Gay couples can also take out a policy.

Couples with young children need life assurance and a will, at least. See Chapter 7, "Protection", p. 76.

Tax

Cohabiting couples are still treated as separate individuals by the tax authorities. Each can claim their personal allowance, but neither is eligible for the married person's allowance (which is double the single person's allowance). Because you are "strangers in law", you can only inherit £12,730 from your partner before having to pay inheritance tax (1997 limits). Married couples pay no tax on property they inherit from one another.

Property

If you buy property with a partner, do so through a *joint tenancy* and take out a mortgage protection policy on a "joint life, first death" basis. If you die in mid-1997, heaven forbid, the mortgage will be repaid and your share will pass to your partner. However, they will have to pay tax on the value of this asset over £12,730. You can provide for this as follows:

> *Eimear and Brian (30) buy a house together in joint names. Neither wants their partner to face a tax bill if the other dies, so they take out a Section 60 life policy on a "joint life, first death" basis. These policies are used to pay off duties and taxes arising after your death. Eimear and Brian need "whole of life" cover which will pay out when either person dies. It will also help pay inheritance taxes on property they may leave to each other in a will (see Chapter 23, "Inheritance Planning", p.235).*

In a "second relationship" situation, when either one or both partners have been married, things can get complex. An alternative to a Section 60 policy, especially if only one person owns the house, is to bequeath the right of "lifelong tenancy" to your partner in your will. The survivor might owe some tax on this benefit. In the case of an older couple, with children by a former relationship, this arrangement would still permit those children to inherit the property.

Social Welfare

Ironically, Social Welfare view cohabiting partners as a married couple in some respects. If you claim social assistance, for example, your partner's income will be assessed by the social welfare officer. Cohabitation also disqualifies you for certain payments, such as the One-Parent Family allowance.

13

Marriage

*"Marriage is a great institution, but I'm not ready for
an institution yet."*

Mae West (1892–1980), US actress

Yes, marriage *is* an institution! The State's tax and social welfare codes treat you differently when you get married — not always to your benefit. Marriage is a contract which binds you to another person, too. That can have a big impact on your financial circumstances. Remember the biblical saying, "In sickness and in health"?

Getting married is also joyous, something you do because you love someone and want to make a public commitment to them. It's a pity to let money worries create friction in your relationship. This chapter looks at the practical issues of money — before and after marriage. It covers these topics:

Saving Up

Many couples save a long time for their "Big Day". Use a *joint* deposit account, preferably a Special Savings Account. They pay good interest, are taxed at just 15 per cent, and lock up your cash! Compare rates at banks, building societies and An Post. Saving up together and talking about budgets now, should make it easier to deal with money issues later. See Chapter 3, "Saving Safely".

The "Big Day"

Getting married ain't cheap. A Registry Office wedding costs just £32.50, but a day in Church plus the trimmings will set you back £1,000-£3,000. That excludes the cost of a honeymoon in the sun — typically £1,500 extra. You can take out wedding insurance, in case your dress gets ruined, the gifts get stolen, or some other disaster strikes. Ask an insurance broker about this.

TIP: You must give notice in writing of your intention to marry, at least three months in advance. Contact the Registrar of Civil Marriage, 31 Molesworth Street, Dublin 2, (Tel: (01) 676 3218).

Property

A survey by *Irish Brides & Homes* found that 25 per cent of brides-to-be live with their partner, or are already buying their own home. If you — and/or your partner — already have a mortgage discuss your options. Most married couples pool their cash and buy their house in joint names. Usually, they both contribute to the mortgage as well. If one of you dies, a property held in "joint names" will pass to the other without legal or tax problems.

A "home-maker" who has not contributed *financially* to the purchase of the house does not have an automatic 50 per cent stake in it. The Matrimonial Home Bill (1993), which tried to establish this, was ruled "unconstitutional" by the Supreme Court.

> TIP: Even if you do not own the home jointly, and/or do not contribute to it financially, your husband cannot alter the terms of the mortgage, nor sign over the house as security for a loan, without consulting you, thanks to the Family Home Protection Act (1976).

Savings and Investments

With An Post investment plans, SSAs, Special Investment Accounts, BES schemes, etc., a married couple can invest twice as much as a single person, and get the appropriate tax relief. Both should invest in their own right, however.

Protection

Many couples don't take out life assurance until they have children, which may be a mistake. It is cheaper to take out *convertible term assurance*, on a "joint-life, first-death" basis early in the marriage. You can extend the term later, without a medical examination, and avoid being refused cover if you get ill.

Other protection policies, like critical illness and income protection plans, are a matter of choice. Budgets are often too tight in the early years of marriage for lavish insurance policies, but give serious thought to health insurance (which qualifies for tax relief). A simple will costs only £50. (See Chapter 23 on how to make a will and get insurance protection on a small budget.)

Pension

Many — but not all — company pension schemes provide for a "spouse's pension". This is usually two-thirds of the scheme member's entitlement, plus a smaller sum for children. The maximum pension a scheme member can get is two-thirds of their salary on retirement. So the spouse's share will be less than half their final salary.

You can claim this pension, plus any "death-in-service" benefit (lump sum) payable, if your husband dies. If he retires and starts drawing a pension, you won't get the spouse's pension too. But if you split up, you may have a claim on part of his pension.

If your husband dies, you can also claim a contributory or non-contributory widow's pension from Social Welfare, depending on his/your PRSI contribution records, and your financial situation.

Women should look after their own pensions, as well, and not just rely on their partner or the State. Independence is healthy.

Tax

You must tell the Revenue Commissioners the date of marriage, and give them you and your husband's RSI (Revenue and Social Insurance) numbers. You will be treated as single people for tax purposes in the year you get married. However, if the *combined* tax bill is larger than the amount you would have paid as a married couple, you can claim a refund. This sum will be based on tax paid after your wedding, and calculated after the following 5 April.

After the first year of marriage, you can choose one of the following methods of tax assessment:

- Joint Assessment

- Separate Assessment

- Assessment as a Single Person (Separate Treatment).

Joint Assessment

The tax office *automatically* puts you in this category, unless you request otherwise. Most couples prefer it, because it lets them allocate tax *reliefs* as they see fit. If you are the only person with a taxable income, you pay less tax by using up your partner's reliefs and *allowances*. You cannot take your partner's PAYE and expenses allowances, however. If you and your husband both work, discuss who will be the "assessable spouse". This is the person who must complete an annual return of income, and pay the tax bill on your joint income.

Notify your PAYE office before 6 July in the relevant tax year, at least or, better still, before the tax year starts. If you don't nominate an "assessable spouse", the Revenue Commissioners will pick the person with the highest income. If you married before 6 April 1993, your husband will be picked automatically.

You can opt for joint assessment even if one person is self-employed or unemployed.

Separate Assessment

With this option, you are independent of your spouse for tax purposes. You submit your annual return, as normal, but can send in a single return with the combined income, if you wish. You divide some allowances between you, like the married person's allowance, age allowance (for people aged 65 or over), but keep your PAYE and expenses allowances. If one person is on a lower tax rate or just earns less, some of their allowances may be transferred to the other.

Separate assessment must be claimed in writing, by either spouse, by 6 July in the relevant tax year. It cannot be backdated, and lasts until it is withdrawn.

Assessment as a Single Person (Separate Treatment)

Under this option, both of you are treated as single people for tax purposes. You are taxed on your income, based on your allowances, and must complete your own return. You cannot transfer allowances to your husband, or vice versa. You can claim separate treatment by writing to the tax office, and will be taxed on this basis until you withdraw the request.

You will probably pay a bit more tax if you choose this option, as you cannot transfer allowances to your husband — or vice versa.

> TIP: A tricky area this. Talk to a trusted accountant.

Social Welfare

Married couples are treated as a unit by Social Welfare. If you apply for a means-tested payment or allowance, for example, your husband's income will be taken into account. This does not happen if you apply for a PRSI-based payment. Provided you have made the stipulated number of contributions, you can claim any contributory payment or benefit — ranging from sickness benefit to a pension — regardless of your spouse's income. See Appendix B, p. 252, for social welfare entitlements.

14

Children

You have a new baby. Or, maybe you're planning a family. Perhaps you have children already, but worry about school fees, life assurance or other money problems. This chapter will help. It covers:

Other chapters deal with child-related issues. The next chapter looks at childcare options. See also chapters on "Flexi-work", "Education" and "Protection".

COST OF A CHILD?

It depends what paper you read. *The Cost of a Child,* Combat Poverty's 1994 report, estimated the basic cost of rearing a child at £1,500 per year, or £2,000 with "extras", like educational courses, summer trips, etc. That makes £36,000 before your child starts college at age 18, or even gets tennis lessons! *The Sunday Telegraph* guesstimated the rearing cost at £100,000 and ASDA, the UK supermarket chain, recently calculated that a child will set you back £24,500, at least, from age 16 to leaving college. Factor in higher college fees, and ASDA's estimate rises to £66,000.

Many low-income families and single parents spend much less, and still do a fine job, but these figures underscore the *potential* cost. If you are a working woman, start financial planning before your baby arrives. The next step is to sort out your maternity payments and leave (if you are returning to work). Then, run through a "protection" checklist as soon as baby arrives.

PRE-FAMILY PLANNING

Becoming a parent can have a dramatic impact on a woman's income, career and pension prospects. Ideally, you should maximise pension contributions before starting a family (see Chapter 20, "Pension Planning"). If you plan to take a career break, see Chapter 18 and talk to a good financial advisor.

TIP: You can take out a special insurance policy in case you have twins or more! Talk to your insurance broker.

MATERNITY BENEFIT

If you have a full-time job, work more than eight hours a week as a PAYE worker, or are self-employed and have enough PRSI credits, you can claim maternity benefit. It is a non-means tested Social Welfare payment, paid for 14 weeks, by cheque, every week. The same rate applies for adoptive benefit, paid for ten weeks only.

The weekly rate is 70 per cent of your average "reckonable" earnings in the "relevant" tax year (see below). Benefit ranges from £75.70 (£82.30 from June 1997) to £162.80 per week, and you get the top rate on any salary of £11,350 or more. Your employer may top up your income, but is not obliged to.

How to Claim MB

You should apply on an MB10 form at least 10 weeks before the baby is due. In order to qualify, you must:

- Have paid at least 39 PRSI contributions in the 12 months immediately before the first day of your maternity leave, or

- Have paid 39 weeks since you first started working and have 39 weeks' PRSI paid or credited in the relevant income-tax year. If your maternity leave starts in July 1997, the relevant tax year is 1995/96 (which ended on 5 April 1996).

- Stop work at least four weeks before the baby is due, or else risk losing the benefit. You can take ten weeks' paid leave after the birth.

NOTE: If in doubt, ask your employer or Social Welfare.

Maternity/Adoptive Leave

Mothers can take further unpaid leave of four weeks. Thanks to an EU accord, both fathers and mothers will be able to take up to three months' paid "parental leave". The benefit will be based on Social Welfare levels, and may be introduced during 1997. Some employers are resisting this, however.

Self-employed and Low-income Workers

Thanks to the 1997 Budget self-employed women can also claim MB.

Low-salary earners can claim the equivalent of disability benefit, instead of MB, if the 70 per cent rule would give them under £75.70/£82.30 per week. Disability benefit is £64.50 per week, increasing to £67.50 in June 1997, plus £13.20 per child. Social Welfare will assess your income automatically, and pay you DB if it brings you above the £75.70/£82.30 threshold. The payment is still called maternity benefit, however.

You may also be able to claim an extra £38.50 per week (rising to £40) for your husband/partner if they are an "adult dependant". They must be:

- Earning less than £60 per week, before tax, or

- Unemployed, and not claiming a Social Welfare or Health Board payment.

Women on a widows' pension, or drawing Lone Parents' Allowance or Deserted Wives' Benefit/Allowance, get reduced maternity benefit.

TIP: Just having a baby is expensive. Medical insurance pays costs of up to £600 (see p. 66 "Your Health", on your entitlements), but try to save regularly before the baby arrives. You can use this cash for fitting out the baby's room, etc.

FAMILY FINANCIAL PLANNING

When baby arrives, you need to review your protection and savings plans. This checklist may help:

Do you have?

- A will ☐

- Life assurance ☐

- Medical insurance ☐

- Permanent health insurance ☐

- Regular savings plan ☐

- Hospital cash plan ☐

What Do You Need?

These are ranked by priority. For information on each topic, see the Health and Protection chapters. Making a will (cost £50 min.) and taking out life assurance (£10 per month for £100,000 cover, rising with age) are *musts* for new parents. A 20-year convertible term life assurance policy is cheap and flexible. Insure both partners, even if one is a home-maker. It costs about £370 per week to replace that person's work with paid help, according to a UK insurer.

See also Chapter 7, p. 79, to see how three women meet their protection needs.

CHILD BENEFIT

After the baby is born, you are entitled to tax-free child benefit until the child is aged 16. That rises to 18 if he or she is in full-time education, on a FÁS course, or is physically or mentally handicapped. The monthly rates are:

	1996/97	1997/98
One child	£29	£30
Two children	£58	£60
Three children	£92	£99
Four children	£102	£138
Five children	£160	£177

Child benefit can be claimed on the first Tuesday of the month after the baby is born. Thanks to the 1996 Budget, parents of twins get a £500 "grant" when they are born, and an extra £500 when they reach 4 and 12.

Child benefit is not means-tested (based on your income). If you on a low income, you may be entitled to other Social Welfare benefits, like Family Income Supplement (see Appendix B, p.255). Ask at your local Social Welfare office, or ring the FIS helplines (01) 704 3482, (01) 704 3483 or (043) 45211.

SAVINGS PLANS

Education is expensive, even though college and university fees were scrapped in 1996/97. Chapter 18, "Education", looks at the cost of third-level education, grants etc. This section covers long term savings to help meet these expenses.

Most parents have to take out a regular savings plan, unless they can lock up a lump sum for 15 years or more. Regular savers have three main options.

- A high-yielding regular savings plan at An Post, ACC-BANK etc.

- A "With Profits" investment plan

- A unit-linked investment plan

An Post & ACCBANK

Childcare Plus, An Post's educational savings Plan, is a long term investment. Like ACCBANK's Educational Investment Plan, it is risk-free.

With Childcare Plus, you must lodge your monthly child benefit cheque directly into the account by "direct credit" and lock it up for five years. It starts earning interest, paying 35 per cent after year six. You can then leave the nest egg at An Post to earn more interest, or withdraw it and take a tax-free lump sum.

ACCBANK's Education plan requires a minimum £50 monthly payment (by standing order). Interest is paid annually, and fixed at the outset. You can withdraw the cash at any stage, without penalty, but interest is liable to 26 per cent tax.

"With Profits" Plan

These are sold by life assurance companies, see p. 220. They offer some capital guarantees, and are slightly safer than unit-linked plans. They are a long term investment (10 years minimum) and are liable to heavy penalties if encashed early. The minimum monthly payment is usually £30 but some companies, like the Equitable Life, accept smaller sums.

Unit-linked Plan

These plans invest in the stock market, and can make dramatic gains and losses (see p. 218). They are long term investments (10–15 years, minimum) and are not suitable if you dislike risk. Regular savers must invest about £30 a month. Plans with low up-front charges (sometimes called PEPs) give better value in the early years. Tell the salesman/company you want one of these.

Lump-Sum Savings

What if you can afford to invest a lump sum? Or if a family member offers to put away £5,000 for one of your children? Over the long term — 15 years or more — bank and building society deposits are a bad choice, as returns may barely keep pace with inflation. Financial advisors often recommend riskier options, which invest in the stock market, because they offer better potential for long-term growth.

You can invest a lump sum (called a single premium) in a "with profits" or unit-linked investment plan. The maximum broker commission charge is 5 per cent, which is much smaller than the up-front charges on a regular plan. Because of this, single premium plans give a better early encashment value but they are not risk-free. You must invest around £3,000 in a single premium plan, but some companies take less. Get good advice from several trusted experts and beware of fraudsters. See Chapter 22.

CHILDREN'S SAVINGS ACCOUNTS

Encourage your children to start saving when they are young. Thrift is a good habit!

Several financial institutions have child-friendly savings accounts, including Ulster Bank, AIB Bank, the Irish Permanent and An Post. These accounts often pay very low returns, and interest is taxed at 26 per cent. Don't park large sums of money in them; use An Post's Savings Bonds or Savings Certificates instead.

SINGLE PARENTHOOD

Nearly one in four children are born outside marriage and many parents — usually women — rear their children with little help from a partner. Financial demands are even more pressing for single parents. So, too, is the need for a will, protection insurance and an affordable, flexible savings plan. You can get good protection on a small budget, especially from low-cost institutions like the credit union and An Post.

Claim all the social welfare payments you are entitled to. Ask about these at your local social welfare office, or a Citizen's Information Centre (CIC). Both are listed in the phone book.

One-Parent Family Payment

Of the 50,000-plus single parents in Ireland, many rely on social welfare. Thanks to the new "one-parent family" payment, you can claim State payment *and* work part-time — thus escaping a poverty trap. Recipients (men or women) can earn up to £6,000 a year, or £115 a week and still claim the full payment. If you earn between £6,000 and £12,000 pa the payment is reduced. The first £2,000 of your savings are exempt from the means-test.

The maximum payment is £64.50 (£67.50 from June '97) for yourself, plus £15.20 per dependent child. This payment was introduced in January 1997, and replaces all existing lone parent allowances.

Networking

Single parents can get support and information from many organisations, especially voluntary groups like Gingerbread (the single parents' association).

NOTE: You can seek maintenance for your child through the courts, even if you are not married to your partner. Separation and divorce are covered in Chapter 16. If you are separated from your partner and have joint custody of the children, both partners may claim the appropriate tax and social welfare benefits.

COPING WITH DISABILITY

Financial planning is crucial if your child is born with, or develops, a disability. Take out enough life assurance cover on the lives of both parents, if possible. A mixture of "term" assurance and "whole of life" cover may be appropriate if you want the policy to pay out whenever you die.

By setting up a trust, you can ensure that this money is handled wisely, by "trustees", in the event of your death. Typically, parents nominate a family member and at least one "professional" trustee, perhaps a solicitor, to oversee the trust. Setting up a trust costs £500 to £2,000 or more, but it can ensure that your child is looked after. You can arrange accommodation and discretionary payments for your child without jeopardising their entitlement to State support, like means-tested Disability Benefit. Trusts are complex and have major tax and legal implications, so get expert advice.

As a parent of an incapacitated child, you can also claim an extra yearly tax allowance of £700. Many disabled children grow up to lead full and productive adult lives. All you can do, as a parent, is your best for them – after getting expert advice and support.

Deed of Covenant

If your child is aged over 18 and incapacitated, you can claim full tax relief on a covenant taken out for their benefit. The same applies for grandparents who wish to help with care costs. A Covenant is a legal pledge to pay a set sum every year, and should not be entered into lightly. Here's an example:

Nuala earns £20,000 per year. She agrees to covenant £1,000 a year to her eldest daughter, Jill (19), who is mildly incapacitated. She "gives" Jill £1,000 in July 1997, but withholds 26 per cent tax — which is £260. Jill can reclaim the missing money by completing a Form 54 (which states her annual income), and sending it to the Revenue Commissioners.

Nuala also contacts the Revenue Commissioners. She sends in a copy of the Deed of Covenant, an R185 form and a Form 12 (annual return). The tax inspector boosts the monthly relief on her Tax Free Allowance (TFA) form. Her salary should rise each month by the amount of tax withheld on the covenant. Because Nuala is claiming tax relief at 48 per cent, giving Jill £1,000 will cost her only £520 in 1997/98.

If the child is aged under 18, and incapacitated, a grandparent can claim full tax relief on a covenant, but a parent none. Covenants are tricky. Talk to an accountant!

Parental Illness

Protect your own health, too. Good protection insurance will ensure that your income is replaced if you cannot work because of illness or disability (see p. 71), and it can pay a lump sum if you get a serious illness, like cancer.

CHILDREN'S TAX-FREE ALLOWANCE

There is scope for sophisticated financial planning if you use your child's tax-free allowance. Because your children can "earn" up to £4,000 per year without paying tax (1997/98), they will pay no tax on investments held on their behalf that generate a yearly profit under that amount.

You cannot transfer assets to children to "avoid" tax. Also, if the child is aged under 18, the income is viewed as belonging to the parent. However, a grandparent can buy a gilt, shares or some other income-generating investment. Gilts pay a twice-yearly interest income, and shares pay dividends if the company performs well (see p. 216). Consult a good accountant and/or solicitor.

ADOPTION

Foreign adoption, in particular, is a long and often expensive process. It can cost £5,000–£10,000 (legal fees and travel expenses) depending on the child's home country. There is no tax relief on these expenses, so start saving — early. Adoptive parents can claim adoptive benefit and leave.

CONCLUSION

Having a baby changes your life. It's an important time to review your situation, and make sure your child is financially secure. Points to note:

- Prepare yourself financially

- Review your "family" protection. Do you have an up-to-date will, life assurance etc.?

- Start a regular savings plan that suits your budget and attitude to risk

- Claim all the social welfare benefits you are entitled to.

15

Child Care

"I have yet to hear a man ask for advice on how to combine marriage and a career."

Gloria Steinem (1934–),
American feminist, writer

Have you worked out the real cost of going back to work after your baby arrives? A married mother with three young children, earning £20,000 a year, could be £8 a week *worse off* if she keeps working and pays the child care bills herself.

That's just one of several examples in this chapter, compiled by O'Hare & Associates, a Dublin firm of chartered accountants. The case studies (pp. 144–147) show the impact of child care costs on the take-home pay of women earning £12,000–£25,000, and reveal stark truths about the economics of motherhood and paid employment. Take a look before dashing off to look for a child-minder!

They strengthen the argument for tax breaks on child care costs, to give the second "working" spouse — be it a man or woman — more reward for nurturing a career. Because there is no tax relief, a working woman pays costs from a salary she's already paid tax on. Worse, if she "goes legal" and hires a child-minder, she should pay employer's PRSI at 8.5 per cent on their wage.

The problem partly stems from the fact that most working husbands claim all the "married person's" tax allowances. Because of this, their wives pay the top rate of tax — now 48 per cent — on a large chunk of their income. Despite these realities, a growing number of mothers are staying in the workplace, reluctant to give up a valued career.

First, before the figures, what are their child care options?

- Crèche/nursery

- Play group

- Montessori

- Childminder

- Nanny

- Au-pair

TIP: Get advice from friends and colleagues. Barnardos has published an excellent booklet *A Parent's Guide: Nurseries, Childminders and Crèches*, ring (01) 452 7222 for details. The National Children's Nurseries Association has a list of crèche and nursery operators (01) 872 2053. See also the *Golden Pages*.

Crèche/Nursery

Most are run by private individuals, but a few employers have a sponsored crèche. They usually offer: a full-day service (about 8 a.m.–6 p.m.), half-day care, split-week (either mornings/afternoons, or five days a fortnight).

Costs and standards vary. Full-day care costs about £60 to £75 a week; half-day care or a split-week costs about £35 to £55. These prices exclude nappies and special food (bottle formula), but may include "dinner" and/or tea, for older children. Many crèches give a discount, about 15–20 per cent, on a second or third child.

Look for a crèche with a low staffing ratio — ideally 1 adult per three children for children aged under 12 months. Some crèches do not take new-born babies.

Play-group

If you work part-time, or want a break during the day, this can be a good option for toddlers. Prices can be low — just £20 to £30 a week.

Montessori

A crèche-style arrangement, but with more emphasis on development and creative play, the Montessori concept appeals to many parents. The staff may also have a qualification. Montessoris cater for a range of ages, 3 months to six years. Costs are usually higher than in a traditional crèche.

Child-minder

Some child-minders will look after your baby/toddler in their own house; others come to your home, and may also do light housework. The latter service costs more (up to £120 a week), but avoids the stress of early morning "drop offs". Child-minders based in their own home charge about £60, but rates vary.

Nanny

Most nannies are hired on a "live-in" basis. They cost £90-£150 a week (depending on experience), plus board and lodging and PRSI. A nanny usually has some training, and may take on more responsible tasks than an au-pair but they are expensive — an option for busy, high-earning women.

Au-pair

This may suit families on lower budgets. Most au-pairs are young girls (aged 18-plus) and live in your home as part of the family. Typically, they work about 30 hours a week, and do some baby-sitting and light house-work. They must have free time for English classes and going out. You pay about £40 a week pocket money (on top of board and lodging), or more if you want extra house-work.

So should you stay in work — or not? These examples show the real cost of child care to a married working woman.

WHAT'S THE COST?

One Child

Jim and Clare are married and both work full-time. Clare has just had their first baby, and is returning to work. Jim, who earns £20,000 per annum, has all the tax-free allowances (except Clare's £800 PAYE allowance) as in all the examples below. The first table shows Clare's take-home pay @ £12,000. The "mini-tables" show the impact of child-minding costs on this and higher salaries:

JIM'S NET TAKE-HOME PAY 1997/98

Gross Pay		£20,000
Less: Marriage Allowance	£5,800	
PAYE Allowance	£800	6,600
Taxable Income		**£13,400**
Tax of £13,400 @ 26%	£3,484	
Less: Mortgage Interest Credit	−£728	
Tax Payable		£2,756
PRSI & Levies (Jim)		1,163
Total Tax , PRSI and Levies		**£3,919**
Jim's Net Take-home Pay		**£16,081**

CLARE'S SALARY (HAVING GIVEN JIM HER TAX-FREE ALLOWANCES)

Gross Pay		£12,000
Less: PAYE Allowance		£800
Taxable Income		**£11,200**
Tax: (£19,800-£13,400) @ 26%	£1,664	
£4,800 @ 48%	£2,304	
Tax Payable		£3,968
PRSI (12,000-4,160) @ 4.5%	£353	
Levies 12,000 @ 2.25%	£270	£623
Total Tax , PRSI and Levies		£4,591
Clare's Net Take-home Pay		**£7,409** (142/wk)

CLARE'S PAY AFTER CHILD-CARE COSTS? (**£12,000 SALARY**)

	Creche @ £70 per week	*Minder @ £60 per week*
Net Take-home Pay	£142.48 per week	£142.48 per week
Less: Child-minding costs	–£70.00	–£60.00
Less: Other costs (transport, lunch, etc.)	–£30.00	–£30.00
Pay After Costs	**£42.48 per week**	**£52.48 per week**

CLARE'S PAY AFTER CHILD-CARE COSTS? (**£15,000 SALARY**)

	Creche @ £70 per week	*Minder @ £60 per week*
Net Take-home Pay	£168.60 per week	£168.60 per week
Less: Child-minding costs	–£70.00	–£60.00
Less: Other costs (transport, lunch, etc.)	–£30.00	–£30.00
Pay After Costs	**£68.60 per week**	**£78.60 per week**

CLARE'S PAY AFTER CHILD CARE COSTS?(**£20,000 SALARY**)

	Crèche @ £70 per week	*Minder @ £60 per week*
Net Take-home Pay	£212.10 per week	£212.10 per week
Less: Child-minding costs	–£70.00	–£60.00
Less: Other costs (transport, lunch, etc.)	–£30.00	–£30.00
Pay After Costs	**£112.10 per week**	**£122.10 per week**

CLARE'S PAY AFTER CHILD CARE COSTS? (**£25,000 SALARY**)

	Crèche @ £70 per week	*Minder @ £60 per week*
Net Take-home Pay	£257.20 per week	£257.20 per week
Less: Child-minding costs	–£70.00	–£60.00
Less: Other costs (transport, lunch, etc.)	–£50.00	–£50.00
Pay After Costs	**£137.20 per week**	**£147.20 per week**

In summary, if Clare earns £12,000 a year, and pays a weekly £70 crèche bill, her pay could shrink to £42 a week, after £30 in "other" costs. If she earns £25,000 and runs a car, she could end up with £137.17 a week — less than a married woman without childcare bills earning £12,000. Clare may feel this is worth the sacrifice, and she should be able to find cheaper child care options. If more children arrive, she's got do her sums again.

Two Children

Clare has just had a second baby. She is earning £20,000, and is not giving up her job. Jim still gets all their allowance except Clare's PAYE allowance. She has costed different childcare options — but how will they affect her take-home pay?

CLARE'S PAY AFTER CHILDCARE COSTS (**£20,000 SALARY**)

	Crèche @ £110 per week	*Minder @ £136 per week*
Net Take-home Pay	£212.10 per week	£212.10 per week
Less: Child-minding costs	–£110.00	–£136.00
Less: Other costs (transport, lunch, etc.)	–£30.00	–£30.00
Pay After Costs	**£72.10 per week**	**£46.10 per week**

Three Children

The arrival of Clare's third child may force her to give up a career — even a promising one — for the time being. But as this table shows, the cost of different childcare solutions varies a lot

CLARE'S PAY AFTER CHILDCARE COSTS (**£20,000 SALARY**)

	Crèche @ £170 per week	*Nanny £152* per week*	*Au-pair £40 plus £60 play-group per week*
Net Take-home Pay	£212.10	£212.10	£212.10
Less: Child-minding costs	£170	£152	£100
Less: Other costs (transport, lunch, etc.)	£50	£50	£50
Pay After Costs	**(-£7.90 pw)**	**£10.10 pw**	**£62.10 pw**

* Basic pay £140, plus 8.5% PRSI
\# Includes petrol cost

Source: O'Hare & Associates.

Other Options

You have other options as a working mother, if your career is really important to you. They include flexi-work, starting your own business and retraining. These topics are covered in special chapters.

And, you can always join the growing lobby for a properly regulated and subsidised crèche system for those mothers in Ireland who want or need to go to work. Other countries have it, why can't we?

CONCLUSION

When you look at the figures, the real cost of child care is stark. If you choose to stay at home, or work part-time, well and good. But if you stay in the workplace, find out exactly what your take-home pay is really delivering — after the cost of childminding and other bills. Instead of being "super woman" for £40 a week, you might prefer more space, and time.

16

Separation and Divorce

"Love is like the wild rose-briar . . ."

Emily Bronte (1818-1848)

Marital breakdown is painful and costly, whether it ends in separation or divorce. From 27 February 1997, you can apply to the Circuit or High Court for a divorce, which will leave you free to remarry. Many of Ireland's 90,000 separated people may not want to go down this road, however.

This chapter covers the financial aspects of marriage breakdown. It aims to clarify issues, help you take stock of your situation, and negotiate, where possible. It also explains the main legal options if your marriage ends:

- Court orders (barring, maintenance etc.)

- A mediated settlement

- State Annulment

- Judicial separation

- Divorce

Divorce is expensive, unless Legal Aid pays your bills. If you want to avoid the stress of court, mediation is a dignified, low-cost alternative. Couples who agree a *fair* settlement now can avoid large legal bills. They may also get a swifter and cheaper divorce in the future — should they want one.

You must start thinking about these issues if your marriage breaks down:

• Budgets	p. 149
• Custody of the Children	p. 152
• Family Home	p. 152
• Mortgage/Maintenance	p. 152
• Social Welfare	p. 153
• Tax	p. 153
• Pensions	p. 155
• Life Assurance	p. 155
• Succession Rights	p. 155

NOTE: Your legal options, including divorce, are shown in the section starting p. 156. You can get support — financial, legal and emotional — from many sources if your marriage breaks down (see Appendix, p. 248). Don't just speak to a lawyer.

Budgets

A budget may be the last thing on your mind when you split up, but working one out can be therapeutic (although initially depressing). It can give you back a sense of control, help restructure your life and — crucially — generate extra cash. It can also deal with financial problems that might have serious consequences in the future, such as mortgage arrears or unpaid insurance bills.

Some separations are far more amicable than others. In any event, both of you — together or separately — need to work out a financial action plan. The first checklist is for a "home-maker" spouse (rearing children, perhaps working part-time) who depends financially on their spouse. The "home-maker" might be the wife or husband.

BUDGET CHECKLIST: HOME-MAKING SPOUSE

- *Step 1*
  Draw up a basic budget (see p. 7).

- *Step 2*
  Check the status of joint financial commitments with your spouse. Is your spouse still paying the mortgage, VHI, life assurance policy? Consider closing any joint bank accounts, but discuss this first (where possible). If you have a family business, get professional advice.

- *Step 3*
  Ask yourself: what do I need to live on? What extra expense might I face as a result of separation, such as childcare costs, legal fees, etc.?

- *Step 4*
  Contact Social Welfare, Free Legal Aid, etc. and check out your entitlements. Can you claim Deserted Wife's Benefit or another Social Welfare payment? Can you ear-mark some of your spouse's entitlements (if they are claiming already)?

- *Step 5*
  Think about other income sources. Can you work part-time, or supplement an existing salary by letting a room, etc.? If so, how would that affect your social welfare entitlements or tax situation?

- *Step 6*
  Work out how much financial support you need from your spouse. If you can't get this voluntarily, seek a Court Order.

If you are the main breadwinner, you need to do another exercise:

BUDGET CHECKLIST: MAIN BREADWINNING SPOUSE

- *Step 1*
  Draw up a basic budget (see p. 7)

- *Step 2*
  Discuss the issue of ongoing expenses — mortgage, VHI, life-assurance payments etc. — with your spouse. Don't let the house payments lapse.

- *Step 3*
  Ask yourself: what will I need to live on each month? Have I factored in all my costs, such as car maintenance, laundry, cigarettes, cost of outings/holidays with children, birthday presents, Christmas, etc.? How much will it cost to run two households — mortgage plus rent, two ESB bills, gas, telephone, etc.?

- *Step 4*
  Contact Social Welfare, Free Legal Aid. Check your entitlements. Can you claim the One-Parent Family payment (if you are caring for at least one child)?

- *Step 5*
  Get advice on tax. Can you cut your tax bill by availing of tax relief on maintenance payments? Can you claim other allowances?

- *Step 6*
  Think about boosting income and cutting costs. Can you supplement your existing salary? How? Can you reduce outgoings, by selling a second car (with your spouse's consent) or restructuring loans? Might these decisions have a severe impact on your family?

Budgets are the tip of the iceberg. Decisions about money rest on vital underlying issues, like the ownership of the family home, custody of the children, etc. Get good advice from an accountant and/or solicitor when teasing out budgetary and taxation issues if you need it.

Draw up a list of your spouse's financial assets, too. They include lump sums from redundancy, accident payments, pension assets, etc. and may be divided in the event of marital breakdown.

Custody of the Children

Women should note that the courts are taking a broader view of fathers' rights. Fathers can fight for — and win — joint custody, but the child's welfare will be the prime consideration if the judge decides. You may qualify for certain Social Welfare payments and tax allowances if your children live with you part-time.

Family Home

The question of who owns or will live in the family home is problematic. It is best resolved by negotiation as part of a mediated settlement. If you can't agree, the court will.

If you decide on a judicial separation (see p. 157), the Family Law (Amendment) Act, 1995, empowers the court to transfer property from a bread-winning spouse to their spouse — usually the husband to his wife. The 1996 divorce legislation also permits this. If the property is substantial, the judge may direct it to be sold as part of a "clean-break" settlement. In this scenario, the home-maker should get enough cash to buy another property. Her husband may get some cash, after legal costs, to take out a mortgage for himself.

Or, the judge may order a salary-earning husband to pay the mortgage until the children reach 18 (or leave college). The property may then be sold, and the proceeds split. If there are no children, the judge may order an immediate sale and a division of the proceeds.

> NOTE: A judge can order the sale of all or part of a family farm to provide a new home for a wife and children, if necessary.

Mortgage

The court can order the husband (or breadwinning wife) to keep paying the mortgage, even if he no longer has a stake in the property. If he has left you and your children without means of support, apply to your local health board for Mortgage/Rent Supplement.

Maintenance

You are legally entitled to maintenance from your husband. If you go to court, a judge may earmark a portion of this for you and some for the children. If so, the children's payment will cease when they finish third level education. If your husband refuses to pay, you can go back to court for an *attachment of earnings* order. This requires your husband's boss to deduct maintenance from his salary and give this money to you.

The court order may fail if your husband works in the black economy, or switches jobs. You can seek an order if he works abroad.

Social Welfare

From January 1997, a wife (or husband) who is left with custody of the children can claim Deserted Spouse's Benefit if either has sufficient PRSI credits. The weekly rate is £68.10 (£71.10 from June 1997), plus £17 per dependant child. If you do not have enough PRSI credits *but* satisfy a means-test, you can claim a non-contributory payment, either the One-Parent Family payment or Deserted Wife's Allowance. The rates are lower; £64.50 (£67.50 from June), and £15.20 per dependent child.

You do not have to prove "desertion" to claim these payments, but may lose your entitlement if you start living with a new partner.

> NOTE: Your spouse can claim Family Income Supplement (see p. 255), if he/she supports you financially. See Divorce section for social welfare rights after remarriage.

Tax

If you separate amicably, without an enforceable legal agreement, maintenance payments are seen as voluntary. The provider cannot claim a tax deduction, and the recipient is not assessed for tax on the income.

If you end your marriage with a mediated settlement (endorsed by the court) or a judicial separation, you are deemed to be officially separated. You can choose to be taxed in one of two ways:

- Single assessment

- Joint basis.

Single Assessment (called separate treatment)

Here's how it works:

> *Seán and Rita have reached a mediated settlement. They have no children. Seán pays Rita £5,000 in maintenance per year, but deducts this from his income and pays less tax and levies. Rita will probably have to pay tax, PRSI and levies on this money — so she's being short-changed. Both get their single person's allowance, but neither can claim the married person's allowance and they cannot transfer unused tax allowances to each another. If they had a child, Sean's payments to the child would not be tax-deductible.*

Joint Basis

Here's another example:

> *Mary and Jim get a judicial separation in the Circuit Court. Jim has been ordered to pay Mary £10,000 per year for the maintenance of herself and their three children. This will supplement Mary's part-time income.*
>
> *The couple tell the Revenue Commissioners they want to stay taxed on a joint basis. They submit their tax return separately, and claim their personal allowances and reliefs as a single person, but Jim can take up Mary's unused tax allowances and tax band benefits. He gets no tax relief on the maintenance to his wife and children, and Mary is not taxed on what she gets.*

TIP: Couples who divorce can also opt for joint assessment, provided both live in Ireland and neither spouse remarries. They cannot claim the one-parent's tax allowance, however.

Capital Taxes

If you split up with your husband, and do not get a judicial separation or divorce, you can receive property from him and pay no Capital Acquisitions Tax or Stamp Duty because you are still legally married. If you divorce, you are also exempt from CAT and duty on any property received from him arising from a court order.

Pension

The Family Law Act allows the courts to take part of a breadwinner's company pension and give it to his wife (or husband, if she is the main breadwinner).

This is done with a "pension adjustment order". The order can *split* the pension, enabling the home-maker (usually a wife) to remove money from the scheme, if she wishes. The cash must be reinvested in another pension fund, or bond, and is out of reach until retirement. If she remarries, the pension is still hers.

Alternatively, the court can order that the pension be *ear-marked*. The wife's part remains in the company pension scheme and is designated as hers, but she loses it if she remarries. Get advice on this.

Life Assurance

A court may order a breadwinning spouse to take out a life assurance policy for the benefit of the home-maker spouse and their children.

Succession Rights

If you get a judicial separation (which legally ends your marriage but does not let you remarry) the court will probably "extinguish" your succession rights. In other words, if he dies you will not automatically inherit property from him, and vice versa.

This permits a clean break settlement. Note that a "wife" cannot be written out of a will, *unless* her succession rights are extinguished by court (see also p. 234).

Divorce also extinguishes those rights. However, the State has promised that any court granting a divorce can (through "property adjustment orders") make provision for a dependent spouse. Also, if a judicial separation was granted before the divorce, and if adequate provision had not been made for the spouse, she can claim on her dead ex-husband's estate. She must do this within six months of Probate being issued, however.

Your children have no automatic succession rights but they can go to court under Section 117 of the Succession Act (1965) if they feel they were unfairly treated. You can take out a "whole of life" assurance policy to guarantee them a lump sum, but the premiums are dear. Financial and tax planning after marital breakdown is complex. Get good legal and financial advice.

TIP: Couples in "second relationships" can also use life assurance policies to provide for each other (see p. 122).

LEGAL OPTIONS

Informal Separation

Some couples just split up, and have informal agreements on maintenance, access to the children, ownership and access to the family home, etc. Though non-confrontational, this can deny a "home-maker" spouse — usually the woman — her share of valuable assets, like her husband's pension, property, etc. An amicable separation does not stop you from going to the District Court for an order (see below). Also, you can still apply for a divorce or judicial separation later on.

Court Orders: Barring, Custody, Maintenance etc.

You can go to the District Court for orders that restrain your husband or require him to pay maintenance. This is separate process from seeking either a judicial separation or divorce. Get a solicitor to represent you in court, if possible.

Mediation

Some couples can reach a fair, negotiated settlement. The usual procedure is to go to a mediator — either a private individual or the free State-run service — who helps draw up a document which state the terms on which you agree to separate. These are listed under "heads of agreement", and cover issues such as: ownership of the family home, custody and access to children, maintenance, succession rights, pension arrangements, etc. Ideally, this is achieved in about six sessions. You can ask a solicitor to translate this document into a "Deed of Separation" and have it endorsed by a Deed or Rule of Court, if you wish.

Judicial Separation

If you can't negotiate, solicitors may have to handle the dispute. Unfortunately, this is expensive and time-consuming.

If solicitors cannot agree terms either, you can go to the Circuit Court or High Court for a Judicial Separation. This usually entails hiring a solicitor and barristers. The case may take years to reach court. When the day arrives, the judge decides the key issues of maintenance, custody, ownership of the family home, etc. Their opinion will be based upon each spouse's testimony, expert witnesses and the children's wishes. Children do not have to give evidence in court. They can be interviewed by a child psychologist, who prepares a report for the judge.

A Judicial Separation can achieve a clean break after years of bitter wrangling. The hearings are held in a relatively informal atmosphere to make the process as un-intimidating as possible. However, it can cost both spouses at least £3,000-plus apiece in legal costs (see table next page). Some argue that mediation is better, because it is non-confrontational, less costly and quicker. Partners of wealthy spouses may be better served in court, however.

State Annulment

The Court can annul — wipe out — your marriage, if it finds that the marriage contract was fundamentally flawed. It might do this if a partner was proven to be homosexual, impotent, insane or had failed to give consent. Nullity cases can now be taken in the Circuit Court or High Court. Those taken in the latter are very dear.

TIPS: AIM Family Mediation offers a mediation service at £20 per hour, to help you reach a negotiated settlement. It also publishes information leaflets. Tel (01) 670 8363.

Also, the Civil Legal Aid Board gives legal advice to people of modest means. You can pay as little as £23 for a judicial separation or divorce, depending on your income. You can access this help at law centres around Ireland. Contact: (01) 661 5811 for details.

Cost of Marriage Breakdown

	Min. Cost per Spouse (approx.)
Drafting of Separation agreement	£600*
Judicial Separation (Circuit Court)	£5,000*
Divorce (Circuit Court)	£3,000–6,000*
Nullity (High Court)	£5,000–7,000*
Protection Order (District Court)	£150
Barring, Maintenance, Custody, Access Orders	£400 each
Any Combination of the four orders above	£600
"Watching brief" based on half day in court	£150
Making a simple will	£50

* Guideline figures only. The higher price indicates the possible cost of a contested case. High Court costs are far higher, for both judicial separations and divorce. Prices exclude VAT.

Adapted from: Dublin Solicitors' Bar Association Survey, 1996

Divorce

This is the final phase in the separation process. As well as ending your marriage (as a judicial separation does) it entitles you to re-marry.

You can file for divorce on a "no-fault" basis (with no requirement to prove adultery or another cause), and must have been separated for at least four of the previous five years. You can have continued to share the same family home, in certain circumstances.

The terms of Irish divorce are mapped out in the Family Law (Divorce) Act 1996 and the process of seeking one is similar to that for a judicial separation. You must issue special proceedings, either a Family Law civil bill (Circuit court) or Summons (High Court). Couples with larger assets at dispute must go the High Court, where costs are also higher.

In court, the judge adjudicates on disputed matters. The judge may not grant a divorce application until they feel that a dependent spouse has been properly provided for.

Costs for an uncontested case, where ample arrangements are in place, may start at £2,000, per spouse, but you can expect to pay £5,000-plus for contentious cases. High Court divorces (and judicial separations) may be very costly — up to £50,000 per spouse.

If you have already applied for a judicial separation you can issue separate proceedings for divorce in the hopes that this application will also be heard when your case arrives in court.

Remarriage

Under the Social Welfare Act 1995, a divorced spouse can still claim a widow's pension (contributory or non-contributory, depending on their PRSI records and her means) if her former husband dies. If he had remarried, both she and the husband's second wife have this right. If the first wife remarries, she is no longer entitled to claim a social welfare pension on his behalf, but is entitled to a share of a company pension awarded on a "split" basis by a court.

The natural/adoptive children of first and second marriages — and those outside marriage — have the same rights in law.

CONCLUSION

Personal financial planning is not static. A woman's needs and priorities can change dramatically as she moves through life. Bear these points in mind when you embark on "life-cycle" planning.

- Financial independence is healthy, whatever your marital status. Plan for your own pension, if possible

- Take out protection for dependants

- Don't leave financial planning to your partner or husband. Work out a joint approach to money matters

- If your marriage breaks down, seek help from different quarters. Don't rush into an expensive, bitter court case.

Part 3

Future Planning

17

Flexi-work

"I don't want to make money. I just want to be wonderful."

Marilyn Monroe, American actress (1926–1962)

If you are a working mother, the arrival of a first (or later) baby may force you to rethink your career plans.

Until 1973, the "marriage ban" required women to retire as soon as they wed. Such discrimination is now illegal, and married women make up half of Ireland's female labour force. Some women still leave full-time work when they start a family. Others stay, because their salary pays the mortgage or because they want the stimulation of work outside the home. So, maternity leave over, it's a case of juggling with a full-time job, child-minders or the crèche.

Given a real choice, you — or your partner — might pick the kinder option of part-time or flexible hours that nurture both career *and* family.

Motherhood isn't the only reason for wanting to leave a full-time job. You may be under stress. You might want more time for study, family commitments or "personal development", like writing that novel!

This chapter lists your options. Try thinking like Charles Handy, the best-selling author. The future of work is about selling your skills, not clinging to a 9 to 5 job that may vanish one day.

Your different work options include:

- Job sharing

- Flexi-time, and other part-time options

- Contract work

- Teleworking

- Start your own business

Job-sharing

This is a good idea, provided you (or your employer) finds a person to split the working week with. Good communication and co-oper-ation with fellow job-sharer, and boss, are vital.

Job-share schedules vary. You can work split weeks — typically, Thursday and Friday one week and Monday to Wednesday the next. Some job-sharers divide mornings and afternoons between them; others work one week on, one week off. The net result is the same. Over a two-week cycle, the job-sharer usually works one week.

In the public sector, where it is actively promoted, job-sharing is on the rise. Almost 10 per cent of Ireland's 29,382 civil servants — just over 2,200 people — were job-sharing at the last count. They aren't losing much pay, either. The example below provided by a Dublin based accountant, reveals that a person who halves her working hours can still earn two-thirds of her original pay packet.

It's November 1996. Kate is a graphic designer with a full-time job. She earns £21,000 pa, before tax. Her husband Des is an architect, with a gross salary of £25,000. They are "jointly assessed" for tax purposes (see p.28) and have split their allowances on a 50:50 basis.

What do they earn, after deductions? How much will their income drop if Kate works part-time, and earns £11,500 pa?

*Kate works full-time:**

	Total	Kate	Des
Gross Salary	£46,000	£21,000	£25,000
Take-home Pay	**£30,141**	**£14,111**	**£16,030**

Kate works half-time:

	Total	Kate	Des
Gross Salary	£36,500	£11,500	£25,000
Take-home Pay	**£25,937**	**£9,204**	**£16,734**

Kate's salary has shrunk, so all her income is now taxed at 27 per cent. She takes home 65.3 per cent of her full-time pay. Des gets some of Kate's unused tax allowances, so he pays less tax at the top 48 per cent rate. His net pay rises by 4.4 per cent, or £13.50 per week. Overall, their income has fallen by under £4,200, or £80 a week.

* Examples based on pre-Budget tax allowances for 1996/97 tax year. Kates salary will rise from April 1997, thanks to a fall in the lower tax rate to 26 per cent.

Source: Fiona Duffy, Brian Phelan, chartered accountants, Dublin.

Flexi-time/Part-time

Your employer may agree to a more flexible schedule, perhaps a working day that starts later, or is shorter, but includes core working hours. He or she may let you work a four-day week.

This is done by negotiation. An employer can refuse such a request, but you have rights too. Under the Maternity Protection Act, 1994, your employer must respond if your job poses a risk to you or your unborn baby's health during pregnancy. These steps include "removing the risk" posed in your job or moving you to a different post. If your medical condition warrants it, you can get health and safety leave under the Act. But you may only get Social Welfare disability benefit, instead of full-time pay.

Say you want to work part-time after your baby arrives. If your employer turns down this request, you may be able to fight the decision on discrimination grounds as at least one woman has done in Northern Ireland. Talk to your union and the Employment Equality Agency (EEA) about this.

If your boss lets you work part-time, for at least eight hours a week, your employment rights are guaranteed by law.

The Regular Part-time (Protection of Employees) Act 1991 entitles you to sickness benefit and other PRSI-based payments, minimum annual leave (six hours for every 100 hours worked, after 13 weeks' service) and maternity leave. Depending on your time with the company, you are protected against unfair dismissal (after one year's service) and entitled to redundancy pay (after two year's service).

Public holidays can be tricky. You are entitled to nine days' holiday like any other PAYE worker. If you were not rostered to work that day, however, your employer may resist giving you another day off, or extra pay. Discuss this before switching to part-time work.

TIP: If you feel you have been discriminated against in work, due to your gender or part-time status, contact The Employment Equality Agency. It can provide vital information and help bring a case under "Equality" legislation. Contact your union also. The EEA is at: 36 Upper Mount Street, Dublin 2. Tel: (01) 662 4577.

Contract Work

What if you are offered work on a contract basis? Fixed term contracts account for a growing percentage of jobs in the 1990s. Unfortunately, it should carry a "wealth warning". Unless you plan your finances properly, contract work can do them a lot of harm.

If you switch to a "Contract for Services", you will be treated as an independent contractor instead of a PAYE worker. Essentially, you are now self-employed and must pay your own income tax, PRSI (on a voluntary basis, if you wish) and pension contributions. You may also be denied benefits that permanent co-workers take for granted, such as sick pay, maternity leave, paid holiday leave (or any holidays at all), the protection of the Unfair Dismissals Act and the right to a lump sum payment in the event of redundancy. See also chapter 7, p. 85.

If you are hired on a "contract service basis", you are a company employee (either full- or part-time) for the agreed period of time. Tax and PRSI are deducted from your wages, and you are entitled to all the above benefits, plus paid holiday leave of at least three weeks a year (if you are a full-time worker).

Clearly, a "contract service basis" gives more protection. It is illegal for a company to hire workers on a series of rolling, short-term contracts to deny them rights under employment law, but some bosses do this.

PAYE or not PAYE?

Ask yourself these questions:

- Does my employer deduct income tax, PRSI, levies from my weekly pay cheque?

- Does he give me holiday/sick leave (on negotiation)?

- Do I work at his premises, not my own?

- Do I work over eight hours a week on a rostered basis, and have I done so for over a year?

- Am I expected to be available when my employer needs me?

If you answer "Yes" to most of the above questions, you should probably be a PAYE worker. Talk to your union, a solicitor and/or the Department of Enterprise and Employment.

Teleworking

At just 1.4 per cent, Ireland's teleworking population is tiny — but growing fast.

Country	Labour Force	Teleworkers	% Teleworking
US	121,600,000	5,518,860	4.54%
Germany	36,528,000	149,013	0.48%
UK	25,630,000	563,182	2.2%
Ireland	1,284,000	15,000	1.4%

Adapted from: *The Teleworking Handbook*

The phrase "teleworking" means doing some or all of your work at home, while communicating by telephone and computer link with the outside world. Teleworking allows flexibility. It removes the need to travel to work, frees up time with your family when you need it by allowing you to work outside a 9 to 5 schedule. Bosses benefit, too. Teleworking cuts down absenteeism, staff turnover but can boost productivity. It also cuts overheads. Rank Xerox in the UK reduced its annual costs per staff member by £17,000 in a recent trial. Setting up each teleworker cost just £1,800.

About 1.2 million people are teleworking in the EU. In Ireland, the concept is still very new for some people, so can you get started? The first step is to buy a book, like *The Teleworking Handbook* or *Telefutures*. Get advice on technology aspects. Think about how teleworking will affect your children and/or partner. Now, give some thought to your personal finances.

THE TELEWORKER'S CHECKLIST

1. Will I stay in my PAYE job, or start my own business? How will that affect my tax and pension planning?

2. Is my house equipped for teleworking? Will I have to refurbish a room?

3. What equipment will I need, such as a personal computer with a printer, and E-Mail connection? A desk? Special lighting? Can I get this equipment second-hand?

4. Will I need a bank or credit union loan to finance these costs?

Issues like tax, pension and investment planning are covered in other chapters and will depend chiefly on whether you stay in PAYE employment or not. See also Chapter 21, p. 200 (Tax); Chapter 20, p. 183

(Pensions) and Chapter 19, p. 176 (Starting Your Own Business). Here are a few points that affect all teleworkers:

House

Converting a single room in your house to an office should not affect your mortgage. But your bank/building society may ask for a commercial lending rate — which is about 3 points above the standard residential mortgage rate — if you turn the entire house into an office. You may also need planning permission.

This might happen if you and a team of people set up a desk-top publishing business at home, for example.

Self-employed teleworkers can claim mortgage interest relief on that part of the house which you have designated as an office, perhaps one-fifth. This can cut your annual tax bill. Remember that if you sell your house you may face a Capital Gains Tax (CGT) liability on that portion of the property. That's because your home is exempt from CGT, but a commercial property is liable for the tax. Talk to an accountant.

Other Costs

As a teleworker, your telephone, heating, light and stationery costs will probably rise. If you are a PAYE worker, ask your employer to contribute to these costs. If you are self-employed, keep all receipts and deduct them from your profits. Talk to an accountant about this.

Insurance

Don't ignore this. Your PC and other equipment are vital worktools and should be insured against "all risks", which includes theft, accidental damage, etc. If customers visit your house, you should also have public liability insurance in case they trip in the hallway and break a leg!

Insuring a computer, printer, fax or modem etc. for £2,000–£2,500 may require a special "home office" insurance policy. But some insurers will add it to your existing contents insurance for nothing.

Start Your own Business

Got a good idea? See Chapter 19, p. 76.

CONCLUSION

The image of a "superwoman" struggling with work, children and her relationship used to be the role model for some working mothers.

Now, thanks to more progressive employers, State support and equality legislation, more women are able to choose more family-friendly work schedules instead.

Switching to part-time, flexi-time, contract or telework can hurt your career prospects and personal finances. But when managed properly, flexible work can be a humane and logical alternative to the stark "all or nothing" of a 9 to 5 job, versus full-time parenting.

18

Career Break: Education and Training

"An investment in knowledge always pays the best interest."

Benjamin Franklin (1706–1790),
American statesman, writer

It's not just your son or daughter you might be packing off to college soon — but yourself. Mature women students are going back to education, thanks in part to "free fees" for part-time (undergraduate) students.

Women are also brushing up skills on FAS-sponsored "Return to Work" schemes and vocational training after years of child-rearing. And, judging by the statistics, many are getting back into the labour force. This chapter looks at a few aspects of education, training and career breaks. For addresses and useful contacts, see Appendix A, p. 249.

College: What's the Cost?

Undergraduate fees for full-time courses at state-funded colleges — including RTCs, DITs etc. — were abolished in the 1996/97 academic year. But students still have to pay a non-tuition fee to their college. About £150, they must pay this when they register at the start of the academic year. If they get a grant, the State pays all but £10 of this charge.

Some students do not qualify for "free fees". They include:

- Students who repeat a year or change course, even when moving to another college

- Post-graduate students (who have done a first degree)

- Foreign students

- Students in some private colleges.

Students who attend private colleges, such as the Royal College of Surgeons, qualify for tax relief on fees. They, or their parents, can claim this. Contact the Department of Education (01) 873 4700 for a list of approved colleges and details about the refund scheme. You can also get tax relief for fees spent on part-time study, including third level students.

TIP: The State's "free fees" scheme also applies to first-time mature students, and those who have already pursued but not completed a course which was not funded by the government. If you are unemployed, you can retain your benefits and study as a mature student at any approved third level course. This also applies to secondary and vocational training courses (VTOS scheme), but certain conditions apply. Contact your local college, Department of Social Welfare, etc.

COLLEGE: WHAT'S THE COST?

Student Away from Home	Week	Year
	£	£
Capitation	—	£150.00
Rent	40.00	1,440.00
Food	32.00	1,152.00
ESB/fuel/phone	25.00	900.00
City travel	5.00	180.00
Books/equipment etc.	—	300.00
Travel home (£15 per month)	—	135.00
Clothes/medical etc.	15.00	540.00
Entertainment, misc.	20.00	720.00
Total	**£137.00**	**£5,517.00**
Student Living at Home	Week	Year
	£	£
Capitation		£150.00
Keep	16.00	576.00
Food	25.00	900.00
City travel	8.50	306.00
Books/equipment etc.	—	300.00
Clothes/medical etc.	15.00	540.00
Entertainment, misc.	20.00	720.00
Total	**£84.50**	**£3,492.00**

Source: Union of Students in Ireland. For 1996/97 academic year. Figures based on a student from outside Dublin living and studying in the capital, and a student living at home in Dublin. They assume a 36-week year — three terms, plus mid-term breaks and time spent looking for accommodation

Paying Other Bills

It still costs a lot to go to college, even if the fees are paid for. Parents and any mature students who want to go back to college can apply to their local authority for a Higher Education grant — if their family income is fairly modest. Under the 1996/97 limits, parents with less than four dependent children may qualify for full maintenance and fees if their income is under £17,460. You can earn up to £22,115 and qualify for part-fees. There are higher reckonable earning limits for parents with two or more children at college. Even so, a full maintenance grant is low: £1,600 for students away from home, and £637 for those living near college. For details, contact your local authority, for example, Dublin Corporation.

If you don't qualify for a grant (for yourself, or a son/daughter) and you never took out a savings plan, here are ways of meeting costs:

- Part-time work

- Bank/credit union loans

- Loans from family members or your employer

RE-TRAINING

FAS, the State training authority, offers a wide range of training programmes. Some may suit women who have been out of the paid workforce to rear a family. They include the "Return to Work" programme which concentrates on personal development and skills training, "Start your own Business" courses, apprenticeships and others. For details, contact FAS at (01) 668 5777. Other agencies also provide training, including CERT (tourism industry) and Teagasc (agricultural and food development).

The Department of Social Welfare's "Back to Work" Scheme allows you to return to full- or part-time work, and still retain part of your payments plus ancillary benefits, such as the medical card. Contact the Department (Tel: (01) 874 8444) and the Irish National Organisation of the Unemployed (Tel: (01) 878 8635) for handbooks on entitlements.

WARNING: You may need to be on the "live register" (signing on for unemployment payments) to avail of some training opportunities. See Appendix, p. 256.

CAREER BREAK

If you take "time out" for college, travel or training, don't let it damage your PRSI record. Your state pension could suffer as a result. The contributory pension is based on the frequency of your PRSI payments. If you leave work to rear a family, you can take a career break of up to 12 years (per child) without affecting this record — maximum 20 years. You also need fewer PRSI credits now to qualify for a contributory pension.

If you are sick or unemployed, the State will maintain payments for you, but if you leave work for any other reason you must pay voluntary contributions to keep your record intact. When you leave work, you get a P45 form from your employer. This lets the Revenue Commissioners know that you are no longer earning a salaried income. You don't have to tell Social Welfare you are taking a career break, but keep a personal record of dates to be on the safe side.

You must meet two conditions to make "voluntary" PRSI contributions. These are:

- You must have been in the PAYE net for at least 156 weeks, but not in the same job or continuously.

- You must apply within 12 months of the end of the tax year when you last worked. For example, if you left your job in January 1996, you have until April 1997 to apply.

To apply, or get further details, contact the Department of Social Welfare's Voluntary Contribution section (Tel: (01) 704 3767). Full-time employees pay 6.6 per cent. The sum is based on their last year's salary, during the first year out of paid work. Public sector workers pay just 2.6 per cent, but do not qualify for some benefits.

Here's an example:

> *Margaret left her job to go to college. She had been earning £19,000. In the first year after work, she has to pay 6.6 per cent of her previous salary — or £1,254 in voluntary PRSI contributions. Margaret can pay this yearly, half-yearly or every three months directly to the Department's Voluntary Contribution office. The cost drops sharply in year two, because she has no income. Her PRSI payments will now be assessed on a "floor" salary of £4,750, so she'll have to pay £313.50.*

Voluntary PRSI credits do not entitle you to Disability or Unemployment Benefit.

> TIP: Planning to write that novel or become an artist? You can claim an "artistic exemption" on profits from qualifying works. For details ring the Revenue Commissioners at (01) 679 2777.

CONCLUSION

Many women are going back to college and retraining after years at home rearing a family. There are many opportunities for second, third level and vocational training — not least of which is the "free fees" scheme. If you want to avail of them:

- Identify a college course or training opportunity that interests you

- Check if you qualify for free fees/training, or reduced charges

- If you leave paid work to become a mature student, look after your PRSI record.

19

Start Your Own Business

"And the trouble is if you don't risk anything you risk even more."

Erica Jong (1942–) American writer

There are many stories about women who go into the bank look-ing for a business loan and walk out humiliated, for example the one told by Anita Roddick, founder of the Body Shop chain.

Roddick's bank manager turned her down, but she persisted. She had a good idea, and stuck with it. And that, say the experts, is one way to make sure that your business venture strides on, instead of falling at the first hurdle.

Banks report a growing number of business loan applications from women. Contrary to popular opinion, they do back women's business ideas with cash and support. But to make your bank take you seriously, you've got to take yourself pretty seriously as well.

This chapter offers a few tips on how to launch a business idea and handle finances in the early years. It intends to whet your appe-tite, not deliver a large chunk of information. You will find useful publications and contacts in the appendix.

The rest of this chapter covers the following:

The Business Plan

Having a good idea is not enough — you need to translate it into reality. One way of achieving this is to map out a business plan which analyses crucial aspects of your project including those you'd rather not think about!

A short but thorough business plan will also improve your chances of getting finance from the bank, credit union, FAS or wherever you intend to look.

Look at the business plan outline on the facing page, which is adapted from a FAS "Start Your Own Business" work-sheet.

SHORT BUSINESS PLAN OUTLINE

1. **The Promoter(s)**
   Name   Address   Age

2. **Education**
   Outline your background, special skills, training, etc.

3. **Work experience**
   Briefly outline your work experience to date, emphasising
   relevant experience, positions of responsibility, etc.

4. **The Project**
   State what product or service you will provide, and where
   the business will be located. Outline the availability of
   technical skills, raw materials, equipment etc. Describe the
   production process.

5. **The Market (in general)**
   What is the value of the market? Is it growing, static or
   declining? State what segment (part) of the market you are
   interested in, and how you plan to target it.

6. **The Target Market**
   List the strengths and weakness of your business and rival
   companies. Why is there a gap for your product or service,
   and who are your customers going to be? How are you
   going to find them, and promote your product?

7. **Finance**
   List the assets/capital of your business, and its capital
   requirements. Do a 12-month cash flow projection and a 12-
   month Profit & Loss projection. (Get help with this!)

8. **Location (retailers only)**
   Where do you plan to locate, and why?

9. **Action Plan**
   List activities needed to launch your project over the next
   12 months.

Getting the Finance Right

You can get cash from different sources. If applying for a bank loan, look for a bank that offers real backing for new businesses. Some banks have special "high-support" units for young businesses which give training, flexible repayment terms and even a "mentor" (business advisor service).

Many women start businesses in their home, and only look for cash when they grow into a new premises. You may find it simpler just to ask for an overdraft or term loan in the early days.

The Tax System

It works on a self-assessment basis, which puts the onus on you to keep accurate, up-to-date, accounts. Ultimately, that's better for your business.

The tax year runs from 6 April to 5 April the following year, so the 1997/98 year starts on 6/4/97 and ends on 5/4/98. You have to pay a large chunk of your tax bill for 1997/98 by 1 November 1997, half-way through the year. This is called "preliminary" tax. It's not the full tax bill, but either 90 per cent of the estimated liability for 1997/98, or exactly what you paid in 1996/97 (i.e. 100 per cent).

If you miss the November deadline, you face an interest penalty of 1.25 per cent each month or part of a month thereafter on the overdue tax.

You don't have to pay the balance until 18 months later, or April 30. So, for the 1997/98 tax year, the final tax settlement date is 30/4/99.

January 31 of each year is another key date. That's the deadline for filing your Annual Return of Income for the previous tax year. So for 1997/98, you'd have to submit the tax return on 31/1/99 — a few months before you pay any final tax debt. But you can cut the tax bill by taking out a pension plan that January.

What do you Pay?

A "sole trader" or person in a "partnership" (see p. 181) pays income tax at 48 or 26 per cent, depending on their revenue. A limited company pays corporation tax at 28 per cent on the first £50,000 of annual profits (in 1997/98 tax year) and 36 per cent on profits above this, but can claim more deduction against tax.

TIP: The Revenue Commissioners have produced a new, user-friendly guide for new business start-ups. Contact your local tax office for a free copy.

Keeping the Books

You can only really know if your business is on track by keeping an accurate log of "income and expenditure". Even if your business is a modest one, open a separate bank account for it, do your books every week (at least), and keep all receipts for expenses. You're unlikely to pay tax on the first November 30 or January 31 when you start trading, but you need to accumulate cash to pay future tax bills.

TIP: Go to an accountant before making your first tax payment and/or filing an Annual Return. By deciding when your trading year starts, you can legally minimise — or even eliminate — a tax bill in the first year or so, even if you start trading at a profit soon after you launch.

Contract/Freelance — A Half-way House?

Not really, say the trade unions. Some employers try to keep their costs down by hiring workers on a "Contract for Services", instead of the "Contract of Service". The latter makes you a permanent employee with full rights; the former treats you as if you were an independent contractor. You are self-employed and must pay your own income tax, PRSI (on a voluntary basis, if you wish) and pension contributions. You may also be denied rights to holiday, sick pay, the protection of the Unfair Dismissals Act, etc. See also Chapter 17, p. 126.

However, you can use contract or freelance work as a way of launching a new business and developing skills. It's less painful than plunging from a PAYE job into a new business idea that may, or may not, work out.

Sole Trader vs. Limited Company

Incorporating your business as a limited company has advantages. As a company director, your personal assets are protected against creditors if your business fails, and you can raise money by issuing "share capital" in your company. You can also build up a pension faster, which might appeal to older women entrepreneurs.

But opting for limited company status is a big decision, not a "quick-fix" solution for financial problems. You must register the company at the Companies Registration Office, Dublin Castle, and pay an initial fee of £165, plus 1 per cent of the issued share capital (minimum one £1 share). Your company must have at least two directors, one share-holder, a registered address and must file accounts yearly.

Sole traders do not have to do any of these things. Nor are they bound by the Companies Acts, but they must comply with employment regulations, health and safety law and tax obligations. Also, if their business fails, their personal assets may be at risk — including the family home.

Alternative Business Structures

You have other options, too. These include:

- **A partnership**. This is similar to "sole trader" status, but duties and financial commitments are shared equally by all partners. If the business fails you share the debts.

- **A Workers' Co-Op**. This can be formed by at least three people, who come together to share their skills, finance and their labour.

> TIP: Workers Co-Ops can qualify for generous grants, plus support from several government agencies. The Co-Operative Development Unit (CDU), backed by FAS, can provide a Feasibility Study grant of up to £5,000, and a wages grant of up to £100 per head for the first year. See also the Appendix for Department of Social Welfare Supports, and talk to your credit union about low-cost loans for Worker Co-Ops.

CONCLUSION

Starting your own business involves a lot of sweat and toil, but it's rewarding, too. You've a better chance of succeeding if you get the basics right, starting with the business plan and continuing with good marketing, book-keeping and close attention to your tax obligations.

20

Pension Planning

". . . And I shall spend my pension on brandy and summer gloves."

Jenny Joseph (1932–), English poet

What will you spend your pension on? If you want a few luxuries in your old age — act soon! As a woman, you have to plan for retirement, because:

- You live longer than the average man

- You earn less, on average

- Your career may be shorter, due to child-rearing, etc.

A woman aged 25 must pay at least 10 per cent more into a pension plan to get the same benefits as a 25-year-old man, just because of her longer life-cycle (see table, p. 185). If she takes a five-year career break, the figure is 50 per cent.

Ironically, many women don't even belong to a company pension scheme, and may be relying on a State pension, their husband or the Lotto to pay the bills. Just 8 per cent of "home-makers" (mainly housewives) have ever been in a company scheme, and only half of full-time working women have joined, a 1996 survey revealed.

Many of these women also have a patchy PRSI (social insurance) record, because of time spent on home duties. This may affect their

[183]

entitlement to a State pension. Other UK research warns that millions of British women face bitter poverty in retirement, and certainly not the rosy future they imagine, unless they take matters in hand.

There's positive news in Ireland. Many women in their 20s are joining company pension schemes, and today's "home-makers" have a better chance of a non-means-tested State pension at age 65, because of a Social Welfare rule change (see p. 187). We are also earning more, and making our own decisions.

This chapter looks at your pension options. Work through the checklist. Don't put it off because money is tight, or retirement seems years away. Even £30 a month paid into a company or private pension plan, right now, can help when you retire. It won't even cost £30, thanks to tax relief.

CHECKLIST

• Think ahead (p. 185)	☑
• Which pension? (p. 186)	☑
• Boosting your pension (flow chart) (p. 198)	☑
• Paying AVCs? (p. 192)	☑
• Preparing for retirement (p. 196)	☑

WARNING: If you have a "live-in" relationship, you cannot claim a widow's/widower's Social Welfare pension but you *may* be entitled to part of your partner's company scheme pension and/or personal pension. Talk to him about this, then the trustees of his company pension scheme or your insurance broker. See also. p. 121.

THINK AHEAD

Now, a mental exercise. Think about the following:

- Inflation

- The price of delay

- Tax breaks.

Inflation

Every year, inflation erodes the real value of your money. If inflation averages 5 per cent a year, the price of a loaf of bread will rise from £0.82 to £3.54 in 30 years.

The Cost of Delay

If you start saving £30 a month into a company pension scheme or private plan at age 25, your nest egg will be much bigger at age 65, than if you start at 45, as this bar chart shows.

ESTIMATED RETIREMENT FUND AT AGE 60 FOR A FEMALE CONTRIBUTING £30 PER MONTH (INDEXED AT 5% PA) GROWTH RATE 9% PA

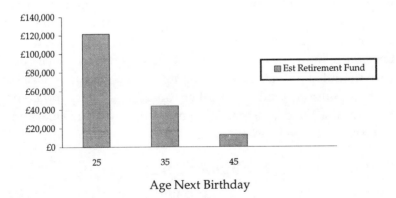

Source: Norwich Union Life & Pensions. Based on 1997 commission levels.

Tax Breaks

These are generous. Broadly speaking, contributing £100 costs a 48 per cent taxpayer £52, after tax relief (see p. 204). A 26 per cent taxpayer must fork out £74 per £100 "spent". Pension fund profits are not taxed.

WHAT TYPE OF PENSION?

These fall into five main groups:

Old-age non-contributory pension	p. 186
Old-age contributory pension (PRSI-based)	p. 187
Public service pension	p. 189
Company Scheme Pension	p. 190
Self-Administered Scheme (SAS)	p. 193
Personal Pension	p. 193

When you retire, your "pension" may come from different sources. As a PAYE worker, you may have a State contributory pension *and* a company pension, contributions permitting. If you switch jobs, you might have money in several company pension schemes. This cash is usually pooled into one fund on retirement. If you earn social welfare "credits" abroad, they might boost your Irish pension or entitle you to a foreign one. Self-employed people can draw a personal pension plan, if they have paid into one, plus any PAYE- or PRSI-based entitlement. Directors of limited companies may have an executive pension (paid for by their boss) and/or the proceeds of a Self-Administered Scheme. All pension income is taxable, and must be declared to the taxman.

Old Age Non-contributory Pension

Your income is assessed if you claim this payment. Thanks to the 1997 Budget, you can have savings of £6,160 and still qualify for a maximum pension; rents paid by people in your home are excluded from the means-test.

OLD AGE NON-CONTRIBUTORY PENSION

Weekly Benefit	Payment	
	1996/97	**1997/98***
Personal Rate		
Aged under 80	£64.50	£67.50
Aged over 80	£69.50	£72.50
Adult Dependant Allowance	£38.50	£40.00
Child[†]	£13.20	£13.20
Living Alone Allowance	£6.00	£6.00

* Increase from June 1997.

† You can claim for each child aged under 18 (living at home) and any child in third-level education (normally until age 22), also living at home.

Source: Department of Social Welfare.

Contributory Old-Age Pension (PRSI-based)

This pension is slightly bigger, and not means-tested. The payment is based on your PRSI contribution record — the more PRSI credits you have, the better your pension.

The 1997 Budget reduced the payments required for a minimum pension from an average of 20 to 10 credits per year. About 4,000 more people — mostly women — will be able to claim this pension as a result.

All applicants must have started paying PRSI before age 56, and have at least 260 contributions. There are two types of contributory pension: the Retirement Pension and the Old-Age Contributory Pension. They have slightly different conditions, but pay the same maximum rates (based on 48 contributions).

RETIREMENT AND OLD AGE CONTRIBUTORY PENSION

Weekly Benefit	Payment	
	1996/97	1997/98
Personal Rate		
Aged under 80	£75.00	£78.00
Aged over 80	£80.00	£83.00
Adult Dependant Allowance		
Aged under 66	£49.50	£51.00
Aged over 66	£53.90	£55.40
Child (full rate)[†]	£15.20	£15.20
Living Alone Allowance	£6.00	£6.00

* These rates take effect from mid-June 1997
† Same conditions apply as per non-contributory pension.
Source: Department of Social Welfare.

NOTE: If your husband dies, you can claim a widow's non-contributory pension or a widow's contributory pension, depending on his/your PRSI record and your means.

Career Break?

Thanks to the "home-maker disregard", you can leave a paid job to rear children without damaging your PRSI-based pension entitlement. You can stop PRSI payments for up to 12 years per child, and 20 years in total. When you are assessed for a pension, your PRSI credits will be averaged over fewer years. If you stop work for other reasons, you can pay PRSI credits on a voluntary basis (see p. 175 for example) and if you are sick, or made redundant, the Department of Social Welfare will pay your credits. You cannot make back payments of PRSI to fill a gap in your contributions record, so keep your record up to date.

Public Service Pensions

Most public sector workers, including Ireland's 43,500 teachers, get a pension based on their "reckonable service" — in other words, the length of time they have worked for the State. You earn 1/80th of your pensionable salary per year and reach a maximum pension at 40 years (40/80ths=50%). For example:

Mary is a secondary school teacher. If her salary is £20,000 on retirement, her pension will be £10,000 after 40 year's service. If she has only 35 years' service, this drops to £8,750. She is also entitled to a lump sum "gratuity" on retirement, equal to 3/80ths of her salary after 40 year's service. So, after 40 years' service, Mary's lump sum will be £30,000.

Source: Adapted from ASTI Members' Handbook

If Mary has less than 40 years' service, she can boost her pension in two ways:

- Additional Voluntary Contributions (AVCs) on a monthly basis through a union-sponsored scheme.

- Purchasing "notional" years of service through a lump sum payment, or periodic payments.

Both qualify for tax relief at her top rate. With AVCs, tax relief is given "at source", so if Mary is a 48 per cent taxpayer, her pay-packet is docked £52 per £100 contribution. The return on her cash is not guaranteed, however, as she is investing in a life insurance-based product. With notional service, she must claim a tax rebate from the Revenue Commissioners, but her final return *is* guaranteed.

As a teacher, Mary pays 5 per cent of her salary towards her pension; other public service workers do not pay this but get a lower salary, instead. She also pays PRSI at the reduced civil servants' rate of 0.9 per cent, plus levies of 2.25 per cent on most of her salary. Another 1.5 per cent is docked for membership of the "Spouse's and children's Scheme", which will pay a pension to her spouse and children if she dies in service. Her spouse (but not an unmarried partner) will also get a lump sum equal to at least one year's salary as a death "gratuity" if she dies. Mary can cater for a "live-in" partner with an AVC scheme — and boost the value of the life cover.

Public sector workers recruited after 6 April 1995 pay PRSI at the Class A rate of 4.5 per cent (1997/98 tax year). Any person with a "break" in service may start paying PRSI at the higher rate, but this does not apply to career breaks. Under the new PRSI regime, public sector workers will get a combined public service/social welfare pension when they retire, in some cases paying higher benefits.

WARNING: Early retirement and unauthorised "breaks" can damage your pension. Talk to your union and employer about this.

Company Pensions

Paying into an employer's pension scheme is tax-efficient — yet only 54 per cent of full-time women workers do it. Many schemes also provide sickness and life cover, at little or no cost to you.

How Do They Work?

In a typical company pension scheme, you pay a percentage of your salary into a *fund* each month. Your employer may also contribute.

The pension scheme is supervised by *trustees*, who make sure it meets the rules that set it up. They must give certain information to the scheme members and/or their trade union. If trustees suspect fraud or mismanagement, they must tell the Pensions Board. Trustees usually get an insurance broker to shop around for a *funds management* company. The fund managers handle the growing pool of pension cash, investing in assets like equities, property, government stocks, etc.

On retirement, you can take up to 1.5 times your retirement salary as a tax-free lump sum, but must use the rest to buy an *annuity* from a life company. This locks up your capital, but gives you a yearly pension for life.

Tax Relief

You get tax relief at your top rate (48 per cent maximum) on your contributions, plus a waiver on PRSI that you would have paid on this money. You can only claim tax relief on the equivalent of 15 per cent of your gross salary, excluding bonuses and overtime.

> *Jane earns £20,000 per year. She pays 5 per cent of her salary into her company pension scheme. This costs her £1,000, but only £520 after tax relief. She also saves £67.50 in PRSI and levies. By making AVCs, Jane can get even more tax relief up to her 15 per cent threshold.*

Different Types of Scheme

A *defined benefit* scheme promises a specific pension when you retire. As with public servants, this is based on your length of service and salary on retirement. If your company pension benefits are *integrated* with the State contributory pension you will get less from the employer when you retire. The amount you take as a tax-free lump sum also affects the size of your pension.

A *defined contribution* scheme does not guarantee a fixed pension. The amount you get depends on how much you and your employer have paid into the scheme, plus investment returns, minus costs. This is worked out when you reach retirement, but you should get a clear *benefit statement* each year. If you don't understand it, talk to a trustee.

Excluded from Your Pension Scheme?

Discrimination between men and women is legal in older schemes, and exists in some new ones. However, a 1994 European Court forbids schemes from keeping out part-time workers if this would constitute sex discrimination. A company whose staff consists of male full-time workers and female part-timers can't prevent the women from joining, for example.

Most part-time workers are female, and the ruling should benefit them, but it is complex. Contact the Pensions Board (Tel: (01) 676 2622) or your union if you suspect discrimination.

Improving Your Company Pension

Trustees can seek improvements in the *trust deeds* that govern your scheme. They can also ask the insurance broker and fund managers for better terms, like lower charges on your fund, but you may have to ask for these improvements. Check the scheme rules, and see if they allow:

- Maximum benefit of two-thirds salary? How many years do you need to qualify for a maximum pension?

- Freedom to make AVCs?

- Scope for an index-linked pension? Some schemes let you buy an annuity that rises each year, others don't.

- A widow's or dependant's pension? Will you have to take a smaller pension to give your spouse one?

- Death-in-service benefit? Most schemes provide this, but it can be quite small.

- Early retirement?

- Portability? Some schemes let you claim your own contributions and any from your employer after five years' service, which is the minimum statutory requirement. Others are more flexible.

Talk to your colleagues before approaching the pension scheme's trustees or your employer, in case they also want changes. You may also get backing from your union. The Pensions Board (Tel: (01) 676 2622) can provide information.

Making AVCs

You can use these to "top up" contributions and maximise tax relief, but check if the AVC fund has high up-front charges. Pick a sum you can afford, and stick with it, or negotiate lower costs. An Post or a non-pension insurance scheme is a more flexible option, but you won't get tax relief.

Self-Administered Scheme

This is a special arrangement for directors of limited companies. Instead of a life assurance investment, you put cash in deposit accounts, property, etc. You still qualify for tax relief and tax-free profits.

Under the Finance Act, 1972 you can set up a Small Self-Administered Scheme (companies with under 12 members) or a Self-Administered Scheme (companies with over 12 and/or those where the directors hold at least 20 per cent of the share capital). SSAS must be supervised by a "pensioneer trustee", who in turn reports annually to the Revenue Commissioners. Investments like property are subject to stricter controls. Setting up an SSAS or SAS can cost £1,500—£5,000, plus a yearly management charge. Contact the Revenue Commissioners' Retirement Benefits section (Tel: (01) 679 2777) for details.

Personal Pension Plan

If you are self-employed or in a company with no pension scheme, you can take out a personal pension. Contributions qualify for tax relief, maximum 15 per cent of your relevant earnings.

Directors of limited companies get even better reliefs. The 1972 Finance Act allows a limited company to offset pension payments made for its directors against corporation tax. The tax ceiling rises with the directors' age, and is expressed as a multiple of their salary.

What is a Personal Pension?

Life assurance companies sell two main types: "with profits" plans, that give some guarantees and "unit-linked" plans, which don't (see p. 220). You can invest a regular premium (monthly, yearly, etc.), or a single premium (paid as a lump sum). If you have an irregular income, choose a series of single premiums; there are no penalties for halting future payments.

Charges are a big issue. From January 1997, the top up-front *broker commission* — just one of many industry charges — on a regular premium contract is now 50 per cent of your first year's premiums. You pay up to 4 per cent for each year thereafter. On single premiums, the new upfront charge is 5 per cent, plus a small renewal fee.

You can draw your pension between age 60 and 70, and keep working if you wish. You need approval from the Revenue Commissioners to retire earlier.

How to Buy One

If you are self-employed, find a good accountant to help you save tax. Use an insurance broker to shop for a life company with a good investment record, flexible conditions and low charges. If you pay the broker a fee, instead of a commission, the charge will be more "transparent" and your fund will grow more quickly.

Women need flexible plans that let them stop and start contributions without penalty. Don't fall for smooth talk or glossy brochures. A *Which?* magazine survey, published by the Consumers' Association in Britain, found that many personal pensions are "rip offs". Get answers to these questions:

Ask the Salesperson/Broker

> 1) Does this pension plan carry any guarantees? What are they?
>
> 2) Do I incur penalties if I:
>
>   — Stop/start my premium repayments?
>
>   — Alter payments?
>
>   — Retire early?
>
> 3) Is a single premium or regular premium contract better for me (based on my income, plans etc.)?
>
> 4) If I add benefits to my plan (life assurance etc.), how will it reduce my final pension?
>
> 5) How much should I pay in, and what *might* it generate when I retire?
>
> 6) What is the plan's value after 5, 10 and 15 years?

TIP: A few companies deserve a mention. Lifewise, the Dublin-based insurance brokerage, has devised a flexible, low-cost pension plan called WomenWise. This permits career breaks with no penalty. The Equitable Life charges no broker fee, which can save you money on a regular premium contract. Other life companies have produced better investment returns, however. Finally, look for a broker who uses the PenEx software system, which compares the impact of charges on your pension fund. Compar, who designed the programme, are at (01) 667 3303.

What should you pay?

It depends on your age, salary and what you can afford. This example, produced by LifeWise, shows what a woman and man, both earning £20,000 per annum, must pay each month to create a pension equivalent to two-thirds of their salary on retirement.

	Starts plan at 25	Starts plan at 35	Starts plan at 45
Siobhan	£229 pm	£324 pm	£521pm
Jim	£204	£292	£464
Difference	12.2%	11%	12.3%

Note: This table is based on a projected final salary of £75,363 in the year 2032 (starting at £20,000 at age 30). It assumes a 7 per cent growth in their pension fund, and a 5 per cent pa rise in salary and contributions. Divide the contributions by half to get estimated cost after tax relief @ 48%.

> WARNING: If you make erratic contributions to a regular premium plan, you may incur heavy charges. Pick recurring single premiums instead. Be wary of building life cover and other "protection" into the pension — you'll get tax relief, but the extra cost will gobble up premiums. Insist on clear regular statements from the life company.

When you Retire

You can take a quarter of the fund as a tax-free lump sum, when you retire, but must buy an *annuity* from a life company. Choose a pension with an "open market" option which lets you shop around for the best available rate.

Buying an Annuity

You give the life company a chunk of your pension fund. In return, you get an agreed income until you die which is usually paid monthly and taxable, as income. This is called an annuity (pension). Its size depends on several factors:

- **Gender**: Women get lower annuity rates than men, because life companies expect them to live longer

- **Age**: Conversely, older people are quoted better rates

- **Interest rates**: The higher the rate, the better the annuity

- **Your lump sum**: £200,000 will buy twice as much as £100,000

- **The life company**: Rates vary, so shop around

- **The sort of contract you want**: An index-linked annuity rises each year (protecting you against inflation), but buys a smaller pension at the start. A guaranteed contract pays your pension for five years, even if you die just after retirement. A single life annuity with no guarantee stops paying when you die; a joint annuity pays a spouse's pension. Get good advice.

PREPARING FOR RETIREMENT

Flow Chart 2, p. 199, "How to claim your pension" explains the steps you should take a few years before retiring.

Other points are important, too. Income from your pension and other sources is taxable, so keep filing an annual tax return (by 31 January of each year for the previous tax year) and put away money for tax, if necessary. Don't forget inheritance planning, covered in Chapter 23, p. 232.

Think hard before you sell your family home. Sheltered accommodation in purpose-built retirement "villages" can lead to complications. As well as buying your new home — typically a bungalow or flat in a complex — you might pay £1,000-plus in service fees each year. Another option — signing over your house to a relative in return for care and accommodation — can create other difficulties. Hiring a live-in carer will give you an extra £7,500 tax allowance that can be offset against income earned by you or your husband.

If you are not well off, and need nursing-home care, you may get a means-tested subvention from your Health Board. The three maximum rates of subvention are: £70, £95 or £120 per week, depending on the degree of care you need. Savings of over £20,000 will disqualify you. Private nursing-home care is expensive, and can cost over £500 per week. Contact your local Health Board for details.

If you are widowed, see Chapter 24, p. 246.

RETIRING ABROAD

If you hope to retire abroad, you've got to plan for more than just sunshine. The idea of spending warm winters in Spain or France is lovely, but the practicalities are also important. Too many pensioners have sold their homes and gone abroad, only to find their incomes eaten away by inflation and health bills. On the other hand, you can draw a contributory Social Welfare pension (and any other pension) in another EU country, and living costs can be lower abroad

You can avoid a lot of problems with proper preparations. Get information from the Department of Social Welfare, the trustees of your pension scheme and the embassy of the country where you plan to retire. Discuss your plans with your partner and family members, and don't rush into selling your home. Why not leave it to fall back on, in case your plans don't work out?

CONCLUSION

If you want a luxurious retirement, you've got to plan ahead!

- Keep your PRSI credits up to date

- Join your company pension scheme, if you can, or take out a personal pension

- Top up your contributions, to maximise tax relief and compensate for future career breaks.

FLOW CHART 1: HOW TO IMPROVE YOUR PENSION

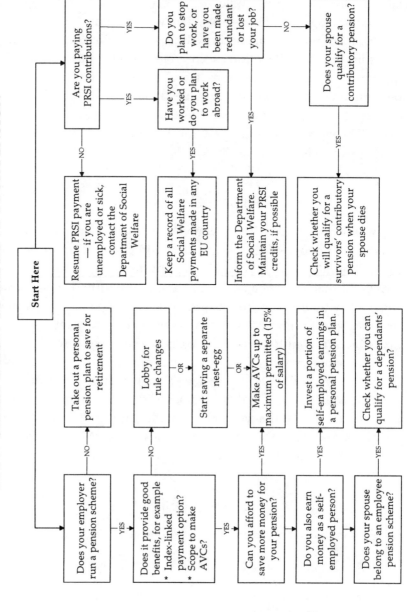

Start Here

Are you paying PRSI contributions?

— NO → Resume PRSI payment — if you are unemployed or sick, contact the Department of Social Welfare

— YES → Do you plan to stop work, or have you been made redundant or lost your job?

— YES → Have you worked or do you plan to work abroad?
→ YES → Keep a record of all Social Welfare payments made in any EU country

— YES → Inform the Department of Social Welfare. Maintain your PRSI credits, if possible

— NO → Does your spouse qualify for a contributory pension?
— YES → Check whether you will qualify for a survivors' contributory pension when your spouse dies

Does your employer run a pension scheme?

— NO → Take out a personal pension plan to save for retirement

— YES → Does it provide good benefits, for example
  * Index-linked payment option?
  * Scope to make AVCs?

— NO → Lobby for rule changes
  OR
  Start saving a separate nest-egg

— YES → Can you afford to save more money for your pension?

— YES → Make AVCs up to maximum permitted (15% of salary)
  OR
  Invest a portion of self-employed earnings in a personal pension plan.

Do you also earn money as a self-employed person?
— YES → Invest a portion of self-employed earnings in a personal pension plan.

Does your spouse belong to an employee pension scheme?
— YES → Check whether you can qualify for a dependants' pension?

FLOW CHART 2: HOW TO CLAIM YOUR PENSION

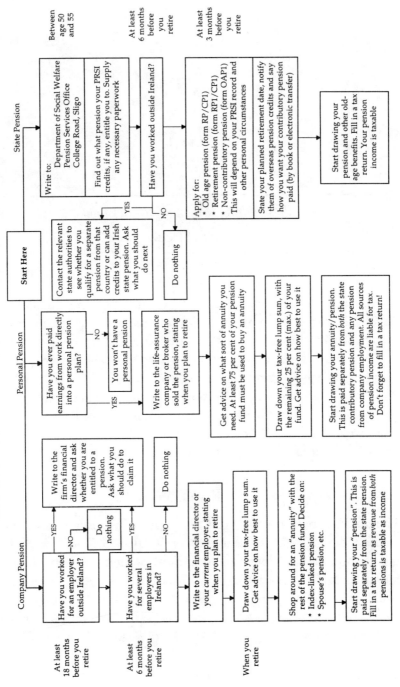

21

Tax

"One has nothing to do now but to pay taxes."

Alessandra Strozzi (1406–1471), Italian writer

Too much tax — it's an age-old complaint. Unfortunately, few PAYE workers (female or male) understand how the income tax system works. If that includes you, perhaps you're paying too much?

This chapter explains how to boost your take-home pay by claiming all the *reliefs* and *allowances* you're entitled to in the Pay As You Earn (PAYE) system. It introduces other taxes, with tips on how to pay less *and* keep the Revenue Commissioners — they who collect our taxes — happy. Whether you are single, married or separated can affect your tax status; see the "life-cycle" section.

HOW PAYE WORKS

The tax year runs from 6 April to 5 April of the following calendar year. So the 1996/97 tax year ends on 5 April 1997, and the 1997/98 tax year starts the following day. In most Budgets, the Finance Minister unveils changes he plans to introduce from April 6 next. This usually puts a few pounds in our pockets, but the 1997 Budget "giveaway" boosted the take-home pay of a single woman (PAYE worker) on £15,000 pa by £8 a week. That's a 4 per cent gain. He did this by altering tax and PRSI allowances and cutting the lower tax rate to 26 per cent. Our £15,000 worker pays lower tax, on less income.

Allowances

You aren't taxed on your full income, because allowances protect some of your pay. They are determined by your age, marital status and whether you are a PAYE worker. Most single working women get these allowances.

	1996/97	1997/98
Single Person's Allowance	£2,650	£2,900
PAYE Allowance*	£800	£800
PRSI Allowance	£0	£0
Total	£3,450	£3,700

* Self-employed women don't get this allowance

Most single women won't pay tax on the first £3,700 of their salary in 1997/98. They'll pay 26p in the pound tax on the next £9,900. Any earnings over this figure will be taxed at 48p in the pound — unless they claim more allowances and/or reliefs.

Low-earners can pay no tax, or less than others due to the income exemption limits (see Appendix p. 252). Also, a married wage-earner can claim double the single person's allowance, but this is usually the husband. Little of his income is taxed at the top rate. His wife only gets her PAYE allowance, and more of her income is taxed at 48 per cent, but their *household* income may be larger than if both were taxed as single people.

TIP: If you're a single parent, aged over 65, or have a disability, you can claim extra allowances and boost your pay. See list p. 205.

Reliefs

You also pay less tax by claiming reliefs, but must spend money to get them, for example by taking out a pension, health insurance or a mortgage. You must claim a relief from the Revenue Commissioners.

They adjust your salary upwards to compensate — called "relief at source" — or give you a tax refund. A relief is usually given one of the income tax rates (26 or 48 per cent), with a ceiling on the total amount you can claim. For example:

Maxine earns £20,000 pa. An insurance salesman says she can invest up to 15 per cent of her gross (pre-tax) salary in a pension and get "full" relief in the current tax year. She invests £3,000 (15% of £20,000), but her salary is boosted by 48 per cent — or £1,440. She also pays a bit less PRSI on her salary. This real cost of her pension contribution is halved.

Government levies are docked from your gross (pre-tax) salary, instead of your net (post-tax) salary. Pay Related Social Insurance (PRSI), the largest of these, is used to pay for state benefits, including sick pay and your future contributory pension. It was reduced to 4.5 per cent for Class A workers (PAYE) in the January 1997 budget. You will pay it on £23,200 of your income in 1997/98, after the first £80 you earn each week.

Two other charges are deducted from your total gross salary; the health levy (1.25 per cent) and the employment and training levy (1 per cent). These deductions add up to 6.75 per cent.

Different parts of your salary are taxed at different rates, so the Revenue Commissioners use "tax tables" to smooth out the impact. Your employer deducts a level amount of tax during the year, instead of taking half of your income away when you reach the 48 per cent threshold. You get one twelfth of your total allowances/reliefs per month, starting in April. These deductions should be shown on your payslip.

TIP: If you start a new job, don't let your employer put you on the emergency tax rate. You might end up with a big bill later on.

CUTTING YOUR TAX BILL

Around February, PAYE workers get a Tax-Free Allowance (TFA) certificate from the Revenue Commissioners which lists their allowances and reliefs for the next tax year. Here's an example:

Mary Nolan is a marketing executive. She earns £18,000 (gross) and gets Benefit-in-Kind (BIK) of £4,500 through the use of a car (value: £15,000, no business mileage). She pays £300 for health insurance and has a £34,000 mortgage. The interest bill is about £2,550 (@ 7.5%).

Her TFA certificate is on page 206.

Mary should check that the reliefs and allowances on her TFA cert are correct. To change a mistake, or claim a new allowance, she fills in the "tax allowances" form that accompanies the TFA and posts it to the Inspector of Taxes named on her cert. If she does this by 5 April, the Revenue will send her a new TFA and her pay should rise. If she sends the form in later, she'll get a rebate. Here are the main reliefs and how they are calculated:

MAIN RELIEFS

- Mortgage
- Medical Insurance
- Pension
- Rent Allowance

Mortgage

Shown on the TFA as "home loan interest payable", this is based on the interest bill for your mortgage and home-improvement loans in the coming tax year.

The Revenue give tax relief on a maximum interest of £2,500 (£5,000 for married couples) or the actual figure if that's lower. They take 80 per cent of your qualifying interest bill, less £200 if you are married and £100 if you are single. This amount then qualifies for "relief" at 26 per cent.

Mary's TFA figure is worked out as follows:

> *The Revenue only allow Mary tax relief on £1,900 (£2,500 @ 80 per cent, minus £100), even though she paid £2,550 in interest. This relief is worth £494 (£1,900 @ 26 per cent). The Revenue adjust her TFA, to boost her salary. They do this by "grossing" it back to £1,029 (£494 ÷ 48 x 100= £1,029). This figure appears on her certificate.*

The TFA figure is an estimate, based on what the Revenue *think* your bill might be in 1997/98 and a predicted interest rate. If you're locked into a higher rate, perhaps on a fixed-rate mortgage, and are not claiming your maximum relief, the figure may be wrong.

Get your bank or building society to state your estimated 1997/98 interest bill in writing. Send this to the Revenue Commissioners with the tax allowance claim form.

Medical Insurance Relief

This is based on the premiums you paid last year (1996/97) and gets tax relief at 26 per cent.

> *Mary's health insurance cost £300 last year. She gets tax relief of £78 (£300 @ 26 per cent). This is "grossed" back up to £162 (£78÷ 48 x 100), which appears on her TFA cert.*

Pension

Mary gets relief at 48 per cent on her contributions. This is not shown on the TFA cert, because Mary belongs to a company pension scheme and gets "relief at source" in her monthly salary.

Rent Allowance

If you pay rent, you can claim tax relief but the thresholds are modest; namely, £500 (single person), £750 (widowed person) and £1,000 (married couple). Relief is given at 26 per cent and must be claimed in your Annual Tax Return, due January 31 each year.

ARE YOU CLAIMING THESE ALLOWANCES?

	1996/97	1997/98
Single Person	£2,650	£2,900
Married Couple	£5,300	£5,800
Widow/Widower	£3,150	£3,400††
One-Parent Family Allowance:		
(a) Widowed Person	£2,150	£2,400^
(b) Other Person	£2,650	£2,900
PAYE Allowance	£800	£800
PRSI Allowance	£00	£00
Incapacitated Child	£700	£700
Care of Incapacitated Person	£7,500	£7,500
Age 65+ (single)	£200	£400
Age 65+ (married)	£400	£800
Dependent Relative	£110	£110
Blind Single	£700	£700
Blind Married	£1,600	£1,600
Rent Allowance*:		
Single Person (under 55)	£500	£500
Widowed Person (under 55)	£750	£750
Married Person (under 55)	£1,000	£1,000
Single Person (over 55)	£1,000	£1,000
Widowed Person (over 55)	£1,500	£1,500
Married Person (over 55)	£2,000	£2,000
Maximum Mortgage Relief:†		
Single (80% of "gross" interest minus £100)‡	£1,900	£1,900
Married (80% of "gross" interest minus £200)	£3,800	£3,800
Local Authority Service Charge**	£150 (max.)	£150 (max.)
Charitable Donations††	£200—£750	£200—£750

* Relief allowances at standard rate (i.e. 26 per cent).

† First-time buyers qualify for relief on 100 per cent of qualifying interest in the first 5 years of their mortgage.

‡ "Gross" figure is £2,500 for single people, £5,000 for married people. See p. 203 for calculations.

^ Rate higher in year of bereavement

** Relief allowed for actual service charges (excluding arrears) paid, up to maximum @ a standard tax rate (26 per cent).

†† The Revenue Commissioners "top up" your donation to the charity by adding 26 per cent. You don't get the relief, but the charity does.

‡‡ Rises to £5,800 in the year of bereavement (1997/98).

INCOME TAX PAY AS YOU EARN

NOTICE OF DETERMINATION OF TAX-FREE ALLOWANCES

The date of this Notice is

24 FEB 97

FOR THE YEAR 1997/98 AND FOLLOWING YEARS

COMMENCING 6 APRIL 1997

Ms Mary Nolan
39 Sunview Drive
Dublin 7

RSI No.	9876543A
Employer Number	3597264B
Unit No.	612

When calling or writing to the **Tax Office** - always quote the RSI Number, the Employer Number and Unit Number. **Dept. of Social Welfare** always quote the RSI Number.

THE FOLLOWING DETERMINATION HAS BEEN MADE BY REFERENCE TO THE MOST RECENT INFORMATION AND TO THE LAW AT PRESENT IN FORCE.

ALLOWANCES and RELIEFS		DEDUCTIONS from Allowances & Reliefs	
SINGLE ALLOWANCE	2900	BENEFIT IN KIND CAR	4500
PAYE ALLOWANCE	800		
MEDICAL INSURANCE RELIEF			
300 = ALLOWANCE OF	162		
TAX TABLE ALLOWANCE	4538		
HOME LOAN INTEREST PAYABLE			
2500 = ALLOWANCE OF	1029		
Total	9429	**Total**	4500

4500

Less Deductions from Allowances and Reliefs

| Annual Tax-Free Allowances determined Allocated to other employments (including spouse's, if in employment) | 4929 0 |
| Tax-Free Allowance notified to your employer | 4929 |

This amount and the Tax Table have been advised to your employer

AAAB & CO. LTD

MONTHLY Allowance	410.75
Weekly Allowance	94.78
TAX TABLE	B
Initial Tax Rate	48%

Issued By:
D. FOLEY
INSPECTOR OF TAXES
DUBLIN PAYE 4 DIVISION 98
HAWKINS HOUSE
HAWKINS STREET
DUBLIN 2   PHONE (01) 6775811

NOTES

❶ The Tax Table and the Tax Rate have been determined on the basis of your estimated income. If your income exceeds this estimate tax may then be deducted at a higher rate.

❷ When communicating with the Tax Office regarding this Notice you should always quote the RSI Number, Employer Number and the Unit Number (if shown).

❸ If you have changed employment your should inform the Tax Office at once.

❹ This form should be retained by you for future reference.

TAX CHECKLIST

• TFA Certificate	❏
• Deed of Covenant	❏
• Medical Expenses	❏
• BES, other investments	❏

Here are other ways to pay less tax:

Deed of Covenant

You can claim tax relief on a covenant (annual payment) taken out on behalf of an incapacitated child or adult (see Chapter 14, p. 138).

FOLLOW UP: Talk to an accountant.

Medical Expenses

Take out medical insurance, if you haven't do so already. You can also claim a refund for costs that the VHI or BUPA don't meet, including; consultants' fees, non-routine dental expenses (excluding cosmetic work, such as crowns), GP visits, diagnostic procedures, physiotherapy, prescription drugs, nursing-home costs, etc. You can submit a family claim (for spouse and children). A large ongoing expense, like a bill for an "approved" nursing-home, can be factored into your TFA. You cannot claim for the first £100 of expenses (£200 for a family) in any one year.

FOLLOW UP: Keep receipts. Get a MED 1 (ordinary medical costs) and/or a MED 2 (dental costs) from the Revenue Commissioners and file your claim to them.

Capital Acquisitions Tax

You can claim a £500 exemption on gifts received from each source during the calendar year to 31 December for cash and assets. This exemption is on a calendar basis, and can be help reduced inheritance tax bills.

FOLLOW UP: Talk to a trusted accountant.

BES, Other investments

You can claim tax relief by investing in a BES schemes, a Section 35 film investment and property which qualifies for "Urban Renewal Allowances" (see Chapter 22. "Investing for a Profit"). These investments are for high-earners who can afford to risk some capital. BES locks up your cash for five years and gives limited guarantees, for example.

The maximum investments qualifying for relief are: £25,000 per year in a qualifying BES scheme, plus £25,000 per annum in a Section 35 film project. Married couples get double these limits if each person invests in his/her own right. Tax relief is granted on "qualifying projects" at 48 per cent, but you can only claim tax relief on 80 per cent of a film-related investment. The full amount of a qualifying BES investment gets relief at 48 per cent; a £25,000 investment costs a 48 per cent taxpayer £13,000 after relief.

You must invest this cash gross of tax by April 5 1997 and supply the necessary paperwork, with your tax return to get relief in the 1996/97 tax year.

FOLLOW UP: Get literature on BES and film-investment schemes, and good advice, from a qualified person.

TAX BREAKS FOR LOW EARNERS

If your wages are small, you may be exempt from tax, or pay less. A person who earns less than the amounts shown below, pays no tax at all. If you have dependent children and are just inside the tax net, you may qualify for *marginal* relief. This reduces your tax bill by 40 per cent. Ask your local PAYE tax district.

INCOME EXEMPTION LIMITS FOR 1996/97 AND 1997/98

Marital Status	1996/97	1997/98
Single and Widowed	£3,900	£4,000
Married Couples	£7,800	£8,000
Single and Widowed (aged 65+)	£4,500	£4,600
Married (either spouse aged 65+)	£9,000	£9,200
Single and Widowed (aged 75+)	£5,100	£5,200
Married (either spouse aged 75+)	£10,200	£10,400

Note: The income limits are increased for each dependent child as follows: First and second child (£450), third and subsequent child (£650).

OTHER TAXES

Income tax is deducted from our salaries, but we pay many other taxes. These include:

- Capital Acquisitions Tax (CAT)
  - Gift Tax
  - Inheritance Tax

- Capital Gains Tax (CGT)

- Probate Tax

- Residential Property Tax (RPT).

Capital Acquisitions Tax (CAT)

You pay CAT if you receive assets as a gift (when the donor is still alive), or inherit them when he/she dies. The latter usually happens if you are left assets in a will or an estate. The tax bill is determined by several factors:

- Whether the assets were received as a gift or inherited

- Your legal relationship with the donor

- The amount you receive.

See Chapter 23, "Inheritance Planning", for tax-cutting tips.

Capital Gains Tax (CGT)

If you buy an asset — such as shares — and make a profit when you sell it, you may owe tax. CGT is usually charged at 40 per cent, but you can deduct inflationary gains from this profit first. You can also deduct a personal allowance from gains made each year. These are: £1,000 (single person) and £2,000 (married).

You are liable to pay CGT on profits made in another country — for example, if you sell Manchester United shares — as these are part of your "worldwide" income. Foreigners working in Ireland can be exempt, unless they bring the profit back here.

> *Maire sells her shares in X Bank on March 10 and makes a £2,000 profit. There is no tax charge on the first £1,000, because she is single. Her tax bill (before indexation relief) is 40 per cent of £1,000, or £400.*

CGT is not charged on: lottery winnings, bets, profits on the sale of a family home (your main residence), a house occupied by a dependent relative, or family farm, payouts on life assurance policies, and property given by one spouse to another. Cars and other assets with life spans of under 50 years are also exempt.

Tax-Cutting Tips

- Keep your "realised gains" (profits from the sale of assets) to under £1,000 or £2,000 per year.

- Minimise the CGT charge on the sale of business assets (shares in your own company, for example) by claiming *roll-over relief*, but you must re-invest in similar assets, however.

- You can deliberately sell a loss-making investment to reduce tax on another gain.

- Talk to an accountant about "bed & breakfasting" shares — selling them and buying them back immediately.

Probate Tax

This is an inheritance tax, levied as a flat 2 per cent charge on the estate. It is not paid by the beneficiaries of a will, but can eat into their inheritance. Jointly held property passed to a surviving spouse is exempt, as is the family home and estates valued at under £10,820 (in 1997).

See also Chapter 23, "Inheritance Planning".

Residential Property Tax (RPT)

This was scrapped just before the 1997/98 Budget, but unpaid tax may be "clawed back" by the Revenue Commissioners if your house has ever been liable to RPT.

The qualifying thresholds have see-sawed. In 1996/97, you should have paid RPT if the house was valued at £101,000 or more (even if you had a mortgage) and the combined "household income" was over £30,100. Parents of young children, the elderly and people earning under £40,000 got some concessions.

WARNING: The Revenue Commissioners have a database of house values and may present you with a bill when you sell your home. Contact the Revenue Commissioner's RPT Section, tel. 01-679 2777, extension 4626, for details.

OUTSIDE THE PAYE NET

If you earn money outside the PAYE net, you should file an "Annual return of income" (no later than 31 January for the tax year ending the previous 5 April). People who hold company directorships must also do this, and face a hefty penalty if they don't.

You must list all extra income sources on this form, including foreign bank accounts, rents, other income (including trading income and investment income). Non-PAYE *profits* are liable to income tax at either the standard rate of tax (26 per cent) or the marginal rate (48 per cent), but you can use reliefs to cut the tax bill on this "other income".

You can also funnel up to 15 per cent of your "other income" into a personal pension plan and claim tax relief at your top tax rate. You can only use certain Schedule D income, however. This includes profits from:

- A trade

- Professional earnings, such as fee income

- Foreign salary not subject to PAYE.

These revenues are distinct from Section E income, which chiefly consists of your salary.

BENEFIT IN KIND (BIK)

PAYE workers can be remunerated in several ways, including:

- Salary

- Benefits-in-Kind; for example, Company Car, Subsidised Loans, Other Perks etc.

- Bonuses.

Your salary is taxed as Schedule E income, through the PAYE system. Benefits-in-Kind (or BIK) are treated differently.

Company Car

If you get a company car, you should pay tax (at your top rate) on 30 per cent of the vehicle's original market value. You can do several things to cut the bill, such as agreeing to pay some or all of the car's running costs.

Costs	Reduction
Petrol	4.5%
Insurance	3.0%
Repairs and Maintenance	3.0%
Road Tax	1.0%
Total	11.5%

Here's an example:

> *Jacky has a brand-new £15,000 company car. She should pay £2,160 tax on this (£4,500 @ 48%) but she opts to pay all the car's running costs. So instead of paying tax on 30 per cent of the car's value, she pays it on 18.5 per cent, or £2,775. This almost halves her tax bill to £1,332.*

If you are a sales representative who travels at least 5,000 work-related miles a year, and spends 70 per cent of your time away from the business premises, you can cut the BIK charge by up to 20 per cent. Any company car user who drives over 15,000 business miles per year can also opt for a BIK bill based on mileage. The tax bill drops as their mileage increases.

Other Tax-cutting tips:

- Claim a reduction in BIK for each day that the car was un-available for use by you or another family member — for example, if it was locked up in an airport car park during a business trip.

- Ask for a classic second-hand car instead of a new model. Because the original cost price is usually low, your BIK will drop accordingly.

- Give back the company car and ask your boss to give you a Revenue-approved mileage rate for your own car in-stead. (See appendix p. 257). This is based on the vehicle's cc and your mileage. It is supposed to cover petrol, re-pairs, tax, insurance and depreciation costs.

Subsidised Loans

If your boss gives you a low-cost loan, you should pay tax on this benefit. The charge is based on the difference between the interest you paid, and the *specified* cost of this money. The specified cost is the interest rate set by the Revenue Commissioners for this form of loan. In 1997/98, the specified rates are:

- Loans to purchase/repair/improve your home   7%

- Other loans   11%

TAX PERKS AT WORK

Some benefits are totally tax-free. Here's a sample:

- A lunch allowance (which must be agreed by the Revenue Commissioners) if you are working outside the office, or luncheon vouchers (up to 15p a day)

- Subsidised canteen meals, provided these are available to all employees

- Rent-free or low-cost accommodation on the business prem-ises if this is required by the job

- Removal expenses, if you are posted to another location

- "Golden handshakes"

- Pooled transport to the workplace

- Your company's contribution to the pension scheme. The scheme must be approved by the Revenue Commissioners

- A share in a Revenue-approved profit-sharing scheme

- Sporting and club facilities (for all workers)

- Working clothes, tools, etc.

VEHICLE REGISTRATION TAX (VRT)

The government has extended its £1,000 "scrappage" scheme which allows a person trading in a car aged 10 years or more to get a £1,000 discount on the price of VRT due on a brand new car. You — or your spouse — must have owned, taxed and insured the old car for at least two years to benefit. The scheme will run until December 1997.

CONCLUSION

Why pay more tax than you need to? Remember, you can boost your take-home pay by:

- Claiming your reliefs and allowances

- Checking your TFA cert

- Making tax-efficient (and sound) investments

- Softening the tax bite on CGT and other taxes

- Negotiating a better deal at work.

22

Investing for a Profit

"I am beginning to think 1929 is going to be a great year for us."

Brooke Astor (1903–), American novelist and executive

As it turned out, 1929 brought the Wall Street crash and depression in the US. Out-guessing the stock market is tricky. Women are more shy of risk than male investors, but what if you need to accept risk in the hope of long-term growth that will outpace inflation? This chapter looks at these options:

Stock Market-Related

• Equities (shares)	p. 217
• Life Assurance-based Funds	p. 220*
• Special Portfolio Investment Accounts (SPIAs) and Special Investment Accounts (SIAs)	p. 223
• Unit Trusts (Irish-based)	p. 224*

Other Investments

• Property	p. 224
• Business Expansion Schemes (BES)	p. 226
• Film Investments	p. 227
• Offshore Investments	p. 227*
• Alternative Investments	p. 226

Note: * shows those investments suited to regular savers who commit a set sum each month, or year. Other investments usually require a lump sum.

There is a "Which is Best" Summary on p. 229. If you want to generate income from a lump sum, see p. 230.

EQUITIES/SHARES

What are They?

Companies issue shares on the stock market, or "float" as a plc like the Irish Permanent, to raise capital. When you become a shareholder, you buy a piece of that company and invest in its future. In return, you get certain rights and the chance to make a profit on your investment. Companies usually divide up some of their profit and distribute it amongst their shareholders. This is called a *dividend*. It is often paid twice a year, and the amount you get depends on your shareholding.

> *Mary buys 50 shares in Irish Football United for her son. They cost £4.50 each, and £225 in total. Irish Football United do well in 1996, and pay a 7p dividend per share (before tax), making £3.50 in total! The company docks 26 per cent tax from this profit, reducing it to £2.59.*

You can also make a profit if the share price rises. Shares are traded daily, from Monday to Friday, on the Irish Stock Exchange or foreign exchanges. The closing prices after each day's trading, plus the highest and lowest price recorded for each share in the current year, are published in the financial pages of the daily papers.

EQUITIES TABLES

	A	B	C	D	E	F
Company	*Price*	*Change %*		*NAV*	*No. (M)*	*Mkt Cap*
	(p)	*Wk*	*YTD*	*(p)*	*Shares*	*£m*
AIB	417	-0.5	5.3	174	680	2836
Bank of Ireland	570	-0.5	5.9	253	487	2773
CRH	630	-1.6	2.9	167	379	2388

Key: A = The current price of each share in pence
B = Increase/decrease in the share price in last seven days
C = Increase/decrease in the past 12 months
D = Net Asset Value (value of company's assets)
E = The number of shares issued (in millions)
F = The company's current market value, i.e. A multiplied by E.

Source: Davy Stockbrokers and *The Sunday Business Post*, 26 January 1997.

Risk

The ISEQ Index, which tracks the performance of the top shares, surged by about 20 per cent in 1996, but share prices can be volatile, reflecting a company's performance and strength and market mood. Rising inflation or unemployment figures can trigger a mass exodus from equities, as big investors sell their holdings and retreat to cash and safer investments. Millions of pounds can be "wiped off" the stock market overnight.

When this happens, share prices fall and the market is said to be "bearish". When investors are positive and buy large volumes of shares, share prices rise and the market is "bullish". These fluctuations create paper losses and gains for most shareholders. You are not really affected until you sell your shares, so don't panic and ditch your holding unless the shares are becoming worthless. Too many small investors buy when shares are high, and sell when they plunge.

Shareholders don't always make a profit. The company may report losses, run up debts and be unable to pay a dividend. The share price may fall, or even collapse, but in the long term, average returns on shares *out-perform* yields on bank or building society deposits (see p. 12). The "average return" hides the fact that some investors lose their shirts, and others make a killing.

As an ordinary shareholder, you can attend the company's Annual General Meeting (AGM) and vote on matters affecting your interests, such as poor commercial performance, takeover bids and appointments to the board. Institutional investors often hold most of the shares, so your voting power is limited.

You may also make a profit if your company is taken over by another firm, because the company making the acquisition will offer shareholders a bid price that boosts the value of their shares.

Which Share?

Talk to a trustworthy stockbroker (one who belongs to the Irish Stock Exchange) and do some research yourself. "Blue-chip" shares — so-called because a company is well capitalised, strong and healthy — are a good bet. Avoid speculative shares, unless you can afford to lose your money. Never buy small foreign company shares, especially if you are "cold-called" (rung out of the blue).

How to Buy Shares

You can buy shares at a stockbroking firm, from an independent broker or from a financial adviser. A small stockbroker offering an "execution only" service is cheapest and probably the best bet.

Stockbrokers usually recommend that you invest a minimum of £500–£750 in each company, preferably more. Typically, buying £1,000 worth of shares at a small stockbroking firm will cost around £50. This includes a £40 minimum fee and a £10 stamp-duty charge. You will have to pay another £40 dealing charge when you sell your shares, but no stamp duty.

The stockbroker will either process your "trade" electronically (through the CREST system), or they will give you a share certificate, with the date, your name and the number of shares that you purchased. Keep it in a safe place; it is your record of the transaction, and must be handed back when you sell the shares.

Tax

Shareholders are liable to pay income tax on dividends and Capital Gains Tax (CGT) if they make a profit on the sale of shares. But you can claim an annual CGT "allowance" (£1,000 for a single person, £2,000 for a married couple) before paying CGT. You can also cancel out gains made on one share by losses incurred on another — but only if both were sold in the same tax year. See p. 210 for example.

CGT is normally charged at 40 per cent. However, if you buy shares in a privately held company which is *not* quoted on a stock exchange, and valued at under £25 million, you qualify for a special 26 per cent rate. It is charged at 10 per cent on profits made in equities in Special Portfolio Investment Account (SPIA), see p. 223.

TIP: If you set up an "investment" club with a group of friends, and save about £20 per week each to invest in the stock market, you can cut transaction costs and spread risk. It's also fun.

LIFE ASSURANCE-BASED FUNDS

What are They?

When you take out an endowment mortgage, a pension or a school fees plan, you are usually doing the same thing — investing in the stock market through a life-assurance fund.

This is a simple way of dabbling in a risk-based investment. You can invest a lump sum — typically £3,000 or more — and leave it there for several years. This is also called a "single premium" investment. Or, you can pay a regular sum — usually upwards of £30 a month — for 10, 15 or even 20 or more years. This is called "regular" or "annual premium" investment, because you are paying in a set sum each year.

You can cancel a life assurance-based investment within 15 days of taking out the policy, thanks to the Irish Insurance Federation's "Code of Practice". But the chances are, you'll keep the investment policy for a few years until you get alarmed about news of falling stock markets. Panicking, you might check the policy's current value and decide to sell quickly to avoid more losses. This is called "early encashment". You will probably get less than you originally invested, even if the fund made a profit.

Many people encash their policies early, and lose money. You can avoid bitter disappointment by knowing how life-assurance investments work and how to pick a level of risk that suits you.

How Do They Work?

Life-assurance investments fall into two main groups: unit-linked and "with profits".

In a unit-linked fund, you and thousands of other small investors pool your premiums to create a huge cash reservoir. This pool of money is controlled by "fund managers" — usually the life assurance company. The company uses it to buy various "assets", like company shares, government gilts (see Chapter 3), property and cash, in the hopes of making a profit. You also get some life cover on your investment, which means that the policy pays a lump sum if you die.

Your money buys "units" in this fund. If it makes a profit, the value of your units rise. But if it makes a loss, the unit values fall.

Life companies have many costs, including the controversial broker commissions. To recover these, they build a fee into the price of the units that you buy, called the "bid offer" spread. It is typically 5 per cent.

This is how it works:

> *Jane invests £10,000 in a "managed" fund as a single premium (lump sum). The units cost 100p each. The fund has a "bid offer" spread of 5 per cent, so if she sells her units the next day, they will be worth just £9,500. Sometimes life companies offer a marketing bonus. A 2 per cent bonus would allow Jane to buy a further 200 units in this unit-linked fund, boosting the "offer" value of her units to £9,690.*

People who invest regular premiums, as opposed to a lump sum, suffer most heavily from life company charges. Up to 50 per cent of their first year's premiums pay the broker's commission. Other charges, including the life company's own expenses, are "front loaded", which means that they are deducted from the first year's premiums. You may not even break even on the investment in the first seven years, let alone make a profit.

Lump-sum investors are slightly better off. The broker's commission is only 5 per cent of the cash you invest. This is built into the "bid offer" spread, along with other charges, but more of your cash is invested at the outset.

> TIP: If you want to avoid high up-front charges on a regular premium plan, pick a PIP. These are offered by Ark Life, Irish Life and the Irish Permanent. PEPs (Personal Equity Plans) have the same benefits, and also tax profit at 10 per cent, not 26 per cent.

"With Profits" Policies

These are different from unit-linked funds, but have similar charges. Instead of paying a profit — or loss — related to the unit value of your fund, the life company pays "bonuses" on the money that you invest. These are paid each year (the "annual bonus") and/or when the policy matures (the "terminal bonus"). Once paid, a bonus can-not be clawed back.

"With profits" investments are a safer bet than unit-linked ones. Gains and losses are smoothed out by the life company, and each year the minimum amount that the company promises to pay you (the "guaranteed sum assured") rises. But most of the profit is often paid on the final, "terminal" bonus. Life companies have cut termi-nal bonuses in recent years. Because most people encash their poli-cies early, they also miss out on this bonus.

"With profits" investments always have a minimum value, which is based on the guaranteed sum assured, plus "attaching bonuses". They can also be sold to a trading company if you want to encash the investment. "Unitised with profits" policies are hybrid products that do not offer cash guarantees.

Where to Buy a Unit-Linked or "With Profits" Investment?

The best place is probably a fee-based independent advisor, who will not take a commission from your investment and give you a choice of products.

Tax

Life-assurance companies deduct 26 per cent tax within the fund from any profits made. You pay no more tax and don't have to de-clare any gains to the Revenue Commissioners.

Consumer Warnings

Life-assurance funds are complicated. Protect yourself by asking the salesperson/insurance broker questions like:

- Do you offer fee-based advice? In other words, can I in-vest without paying commission? If not, how much will be invested in each of the first three years?

- Does this policy have any capital guarantee?

- What are the penalties for early encashment?

- Can I switch between other funds offered by the same life-assurance company? How much would that cost?

- What is the life of this policy (the term)? Does that suit my needs? (Tell the broker what those needs are.)

- How much life cover is there? Do I need it all?

WARNING! If you choose a regular premium investment, charges can eat up all of your first year's premiums. You may get no money back if you encash the investment in the first two years, and very little between years 2 and 7. Aim to hold a unit-linked investment for at least 10–15 years. Or, pick a plan with low up-front charges and/or invest through a broker who charges a fee — not commission.

With a regular premium investment, you have several options if you can no longer afford, or do not want, to keep paying money into the fund:

- Encash the policy

- Reduce the premiums

- Stop paying premiums, but don't encash the policy until it matures.

SPIAs AND SIAs

These are the equities-based equivalent of Special Savings Accounts. Profits are taxed (internally) at 10 per cent, instead of at 26 per cent, and the rate was unchanged in the 1997 Budget.

SPIAs sold like hot-cakes in 1996, thanks to their low tax rate and a bullish stock market, but they remain a risk-based investment.

By law, at least 55 per cent of your money must be invested in Irish equities (15 per cent of which is "smaller companies") by year four. Also, to buy shares directly through an SPIA, you may have to invest at least £5,000. The investment threshold is lower for life assurance-based SPIAs and at least one company, Ark Life, offers a "regular premium" alternative, called a PEP.

You can invest up to £75,000 in an SPIA (£150,000 for married couples). If you have invested £50,000 in an SSA, you can put a further £25,000 in an SPIA. Like SSAs, SPIAs are not confidential investments.

UNIT TRUSTS (IRISH-BASED)

How Do They Work?

Like unit-linked funds, these are pooled investments, but they are sold by banks, fund-management companies and other non-insurance institutions. Fund profits are taxed internally at 26 per cent.

Sales of unit trusts have always been far smaller than unit-linked funds, but unit trusts have one big advantage. Life insurance is not included as part of the package, so your investment should grow faster than an equivalent unit-linked fund.

Offshore unit trusts are taxed differently and may appeal to more sophisticated investors. See "Offshore Investments", p. 227.

PROPERTY

Pros and Cons

Investing in property is beyond the reach of many single women and families. Most of us — even if we have no dependants — can only afford to pay one mortgage, and it's unwise to treat your own home as a speculative investment. The property market is subject to booms and crashes, as UK investors found to their cost, and houses cost a lot to buy and maintain.

On the plus side, there are tax incentives for people who invest in the so-called "designated" areas, and bricks-and-mortar has an emotional appeal for some. Parents may like the idea of buying a house or flat in the city, where their children can stay during their college years.

How to Invest

As with equities, you can invest through a unitised fund or direct purchase.

There are several unit-linked and unit-trust property funds to choose from. Each fund usually invests in a property portfolio, and aims to make a profit from rents/leases, and buying and selling various holdings. These funds have shown mixed returns, to say the least. Unit values in property funds plunged in the late 1980s but rose strongly in the mid-1990s.

Direct investment is more clear cut, but you must commit a larger sum and pick the property you want. You must also factor in the cost of:

- Legal fees

- Stamp duty

- Survey costs

- Mortgage finance

- Repair/refurbishment

- Insurance

- Letting costs (agency fees etc.).

Draw up a list of these costs before buying an investment property. Your dream investment may cost more than you budget for, and deliver less income than planned. Rents are taxed as "Schedule D" income and must be declared to the Revenue Commissioners. They are liable for tax in the year in which they are earned. Thus, rents received in the tax year ending 5 April 1997 will be taxed in the 1996/97 tax year. You can reduce the taxable income by claiming these "costs":

- Rents paid by you (the owner), e.g. ground rents

- Rates

- Goods and services provided in connection with letting the property, such as agent's fees

- Repairs and maintenance costs

- Insurance

- Interest on loans taken out to purchase, improve or repair the property.

You can also claim capital allowances on assets purchased for the tenants, such as furniture. You can write off 15 per cent of the total cost of these assets each year for six years, and 10 per cent in the final (seventh) year.

You can't claim for any costs incurred before you start letting the property. However, thanks to the government's "urban renewal" scheme, you can claim more generous reliefs if you buy a rental property in a so-called "designated area" — chiefly, the inner city.

NOTE: Talk to a trusted accountant about investing in tax-efficient schemes, such as Section 23 properties and areas designated for Urban Renewal. Never buy on the strength of a tax break alone. Remember the maxim: location, location, location!

BUSINESS EXPANSION SCHEMES (BES)

BES schemes will only interest a tiny minority of women, mostly high-earning professionals. You can invest up to £25,000 in any one year (£50,000 as a married couple) and claim tax relief at 48 per cent, but there are tight controls on how schemes are set up and run. BES projects which raise over £250,000 must get a special certificate and create jobs, and tax relief may be clawed back if they don't.

BES schemes suit people who want to cut their income-tax bill and make a speculative commercial investment. You can invest directly in a BES company, or in several, through a designated managed fund. The latter spreads the risk, just like a pooled (unit-linked or unit-trust) investment. If one company does badly, losses may be offset by gains on stronger companies in the portfolio.

BES schemes are marketed just before the end of each tax year (5 April), because tax relief is usually claimed in the year when the investment is made. So, if you invest in a BES scheme by 5 April 1998, you can cut your 1997/98 tax bill. See Chapter 21, "Tax" p. 208

WARNING: A BES investment must be held for at least five years and you must claim the tax relief within two years. Get good advice.

FILM/SECTION 35 RELIEF

High earners may prefer to invest in films instead of a BES. You can invest up to £25,000 per year in a qualifying film investment, on top of any BES investment. This brings the combined annual tax relievable sum to £50,000 per person each year. A married couple can get double relief — that is, invest up to £100,000 in BES/Section 35 projects — but each spouse must make the investment in their own right.

If you invest over £25,000 (per person) in any given tax year, you can carry over the balance into the following year and claim tax relief on it then.

Section 35 investments arise on an ad hoc basis, so contact a large accountancy firm for a current list of qualifying film projects. If you invest in a film by taking out share capital, you must hold these shares for one year, not five.

You can only claim tax relief on 80 per cent of your investment, and can only claim this benefit after filming starts. Other strict conditions apply, and if the project you pick fails to meet them, your tax relief may be lost. Get professional advice.

Fiona decides to put £5,000 in a Section 35 film project set up by her cousin, a promising young film-maker.

Section 35 investment	*£5,000*
Sum qualifying for relief	*£4,000*
Tax relief (@ 48%)	*£1,920*
Net cost of Fiona's film investment	*£3,080*

OFFSHORE INVESTMENTS

Again, only well-heeled women (with few demands on their savings) will put their cash to work outside Ireland. The main benefit of an offshore investment is that income/profits roll up tax-free. The big disadvantage — as the Taylor Group saga in 1996 showed — is that you can lose all your cash through fraud or mismanagement.

Talk to a financial advisor in a blue chip consultancy before putting any cash offshore. All gains (even those earned in an anonymous Jersey bank account) are viewed as taxable income by the Irish tax authorities. You may get higher post-tax gains, with less headaches, from an Irish-based SSA or SPIA.

ALTERNATIVE INVESTMENTS

These can be fun, but don't expect to make money! They include:

- Art/antiques

- Coins

- Comics

- Old share certificates

- Toys

- Wine

Prices are determined more by whim and collecting crazes than by anything else. To make money on alternative investments, do your homework, find a source (preferably cheap) for the item you plan to collect and a market to sell it in. You can get useful information from specialist magazines, the media, auctioneers, antique dealers and other collectors. You can join a collectors' club — usually contactable through one of the above sources — but most members are enthusiasts who take a dim view of profit-driven collecting.

Read up about your chosen subject and haunt markets, car-boot sales and antique fairs for bargains. You may strike lucky. A "mint" (prime condition) first edition copy of Action Comics, which featured Superman, fetched stg£14,300 in a London auction house in August 1994. The seller made a handsome profit and the buyer, a British engineer, thinks that the magazine will grow in value. That sum represented a 25 per cent annual compound return on the original 1938 cover price of 10 US cents.

Most people make little or no money on their collections. Collecting is more likely to become a passion — even an obsession — than a profit spinner.

Gains on alternative investment are subject to CGT at 40 per cent, but you can deduct your annual allowance, etc. Non-durable "chattels" with a normal life span of under 50 years, like cars, are exempt, as are items costing under £2,000.

ETHICAL INVESTMENTS

These are usually unit-linked funds or unit trusts, where the fund manager pledges not to invest in companies that sell "socially damaging" products: armaments, drink, tobacco etc. Very popular in the UK and US, especially with women, these are not common here. The Stewardship Fund, offered by Friends Provident Life Assurance Company, is one of few examples.

Say you get a windfall from a lottery or an elderly aunt. Where's the best home — least risky, but most potentially rewarding — for your cash?

WHICH IS BEST?

✓ Good Option	? Be wary	✗ Avoid
Blue chip shares	Speculative shares (exploration stocks, small companies, etc.)*	Shares in small, offshore companies
BES fund	BES Scheme, film investment	Offshore funds
"With profits" bond (10-year term)	Property	Offshore bank/ building society accounts
	"Collectibles"	
	Unit-linked managed fund	

Note: This table assumes that you have a "nest-egg" for emergencies, have no large borrowings and can lock up cash for at least five years

* Aim to sell before the share price peaks, and don't buy when the price is high!

INVESTING FOR AN INCOME

Some women, especially pensioners with a tax-free lump sum, may want to earn an income from their savings. You can pick a deposit account (bank or building society) that pays interest as income. Or, go to the Post Office.

Here's how £50,000 invested in An Post's Savings Certificates in January 1997 can produce a rising six-monthly income by encashing units. Sums rounded to the nearest £:

Encashment Date	Income	Amount of Money Left
6 Months	£1,000	£50,000
1 Year	£980	£50,000
1.5 Years	£962	£50,000
2 Years	£943	£50,000
2.5 Years	£1,157	£50,000
3 Years	£1,267	£50,000
3.5 Years	£1,368	£50,000
4 Years	£1,546	£50,000
4.5 Years	£1,875	£50,000
5 Years	£2,209	£50,000
5.5 Years	£1,731	£50,000

Or, you can opt for a level income of about £1,300 per six months.

Source: An Post.

Other options:

- Deposit account, see p. 11
- Guaranteed bonds, see p. 32
- Gilts, see p. 31.

CONCLUSION

Women are more "risk-averse" than men, as a general rule, but you have to accept *some* level of risk if you want growth that will outpace inflation. That's something to bear in mind if you're saving for your child's education. Women who get a lump sum from an inheritance, life assurance policy or a redundancy package, also need to invest it wisely. It's vital to get good, impartial advice — from different sources, but be clear about your priorities as well.

23

Inheritance Planning

"Time brings all things to pass"

Proverb

Making a will is important for our loved ones, as we have seen (Chapter 7, "Protection", but that's just one part of inheritance planning.

This chapter looks at ways of passing on your wealth with the smallest tax burden possible. Look on it as another form of housekeeping, which gives you peace of mind and provides for your family, friends, or whoever you wish to leave property to.

This chapter covers these topics:

If you Have a Will

As explained in Chapter x, a will is a legally binding document (or should be, if it's properly drawn up) which states how you wish your property to be divided when you pass away.

After you die, the executor (and/or solicitor) should give a copy of your will to all the main *beneficiaries*. The executor and/or solicitor, then applies to take out a *Grant of Probate*, at the Probate Office (Dublin, Tel: (01) 872 5555; ring the Department of Justice (01) 678 9711 for the local Probate Office number). The Probate Office must be paid an *administration* fee, based on the size of the estate (the value of property held in your name). If the executor uses a solicitor, the fee ranges from £6 for estates worth under £500, to a maximum of £408 (£1 million plus).

Probate takes about 6–8 weeks. If you take out Probate yourself, the fee is doubled, but you avoid a solicitor's fee, which can be substantial. A DIY job is not recommended if the will or the estate is complex or contentious.

If You Die Without a Will (or Intestate)

If you die *intestate*, your next of kin — husband, brother/sister, parent, etc. — must apply to the Probate Office for *Letters of Administration*. Your next of kin takes on the job of *administrator*, and must divide your property in accordance with the 1965 Succession Act (see table below).

This carve-up may not suit your wishes. You may want to leave the family home to a disabled member of your family, for example, or cash to a charity.

IF THERE IS NO WILL

Heir	Entitlement
Spouse Only	Whole of estate
Spouse and Children	Two-thirds to spouse, one-third to children in equal shares. The share of a deceased child passes to the children of the deceased child
Children, No Spouse	Whole of estate to children in equal shares. The share of a deceased child passes to the children of the deceased child
Parents, Brothers/Sisters	Whole estate to surviving parent(s). None to brothers and sisters
One Parent, Brothers/Sisters	Whole estate to surviving parent. None to brothers and sisters
Brothers and Sisters	Divided into equal shares. The share of any deceased brother/sister passes to his/her children
Nephews and Nieces	All get equal shares

For more distant relatives, get legal advice.

Your Spouse's Rights

You cannot disinherit your spouse, no matter what your will states, except in rare exceptions, see p. 155. A husband/wife is legally entitled to:

- Half of their partners' assets if they have no children

- One-third if the deceased partner has children.

This right does not extend to property held in joint names with another person — provided the title is true *joint tenancy*. Such property passes automatically to the other owner, but he/she may have to pay some tax. If the joint tenancy was created to deprive a spouse of their legal right, or a child of succession rights, the survivor's claim to the joint property may also be contested. If property is held jointly as *tenants in common*, your half automatically goes into your estate when you die. Your fellow joint tenant won't get your share.

You have a moral but no legal obligation to include children in your will. If they feel aggrieved, they can make a legal claim on your estate under the 1965 Succession Act.

A married couple should make mutual wills to provide for a situation where both die simultaneously, or the survivor does not, or cannot, make a new will. For example, where a husband leaves all of his property to his wife, but both die together in a tragic accident.

TAX — WHO PAYS WHAT?

You can minimise taxes with proper inheritance planning. Here are the taxes to look out for:

Tax	Who Pays It?	How Much Do They Pay?	When is It Due?
1) Capital Acquisitions Tax (CAT)			
Inheritance Tax	The beneficiary	Depends on their blood/legal relationship with you. A spouse pays no CAT, a "stranger in law" pays CAT on assets worth £12,370+.	When they receive the asset after your death, or if you die within 2 years of making a gift.
Gift Tax	The beneficiary	Ditto, but the tax penalty is 75% of the total CAT charge (see below).	When they receive the asset more than two years before your death.
2) Probate Tax	Your estate	2%	Within nine months.

CAT

As shown in the table above, CAT must be paid on inheritances and large gifts.

CAT RATES

Amount	Tax Payable
Up to exemption threshold (see below)	No Tax
The next £10,000	20%
The next £30,000	30%
The balance	40%

If assets are passed on as gifts at least two years before the donor dies, the bill is 75 per cent of the regular CAT charge. So, it makes sense to start inheritance planning before you die, and "gift" some of your assets. The size of the tax bill also depends on:

- The beneficiary's blood/legal relationship with the donor

- How much the person receives.

HOW MUCH CAN YOU INHERIT BEFORE PAYING CAT?

Blood/Legal Relationship of Beneficiary	Tax Threshold*
Husband/Wife	No CAT payable
Child	£185,550
Grandchild under 18 (parent deceased)	£185,550
Father/Mother (absolute inheritance only)	£185,550
Father/Mother (other benefits, including gifts)	£24,740
Grandfather/Grandmother/Grandchild	£24,740
Brother/Sister	£24,740
Niece/Nephew	£24,740
Other[†]	£12,370

* These thresholds were introduced on 1 January 1997, and are raised each year in line with inflation. The 1996 thresholds were £182,550, £24,340 and £12,170, respectively.
† Includes unmarried partner, live-in or otherwise.

Here's an example:

> *Laura receives a £50,000 inheritance from an elderly neighbour, but she has to pay £10,289 in tax, reducing her inheritance to £39,711. If this money had been "gifted" to her the tax bill would have dropped to £7,716.75 (£10,289 @ 75%). Here's how her tax bill was calculated:*
>
> LAURA'S TAX BILL (£50,000 INHERITANCE)
>
> | Amount | Tax Rate | Amount Payable |
> |---|---|---|
> | £12,370 | Exempt | No Tax |
> | The next £10,000 | @ 20% | £2,000 |
> | Remaining £27,630 | @ 30% | £8,289 |
> | Total Tax Bill | | £10,289 |
> | Net Inheritance | | £39,711 |
>
> *Laura can work out this sum quite easily. The calculations are more complex if she gets a gift or inheritance from another person. She should ask an accountant or solicitor specialising in this area how much she owes.*

WARNING: The Revenue Commissioners view many things as gifts, including cash, jewellery, a car, the transfer of house or lands, the use of a house etc.

Tips for Cutting CAT

- Give away the asset before you die

- Take out a Section 60 life policy to pay taxes and charges arising on the death of you, or your spouse

- Spread your generosity, keeping gifts/inheritances close to the tax threshold for each beneficiary

- Leave money to charity (it's tax-free)

- Gift cash for the support, maintenance and education your children and/or dependent relatives. That's tax-free as well.

Probate Tax

Unlike CAT, probate tax is levied at a flat 2 per cent on the estate itself. All assets (with the exception of those listed below) are subject to this tax. Probate tax is not directly paid by the beneficiaries of a will, but eat into the value of the dead person's assets. It may force a beneficiary of the will to sell an asset — such as a large house — to pay the tax debt.

Spouses are exempt from Probate tax, as is the family home (if a dependent child receives it) and estates valued at under £10,820 (1997).

Tips for Cutting Probate Tax

- Put the property in joint names (joint tenancy)

- Take out a life assurance policy to cover charges arising on the estate when you die (see "Section 60" below)

- Pass on the asset as a gift before you die.

Pay less tax with Section 60

Remembering someone in your will can give the "lucky" person a tax problem — as Laura's example on p. 237 shows. If Laura had received a house, and not a cash gift, she might have been forced to sell it. Tax can create big problems for separated people in "second" relationships who have low inheritance tax thresholds, because they are *strangers-in-law*.

Here's an example:

Mark and Amy have two children. They aren't married, but they have a mortgage in joint names on their £90,000 house. Mark dies without a will. His share of the house passes automatically to Amy and the loan is repaid, thanks to their mortgage protection policy. Amy pays no probate tax because the house was in joint names and didn't go into Mark's estate. But because she was not related or married to Mark, she must pay CAT on her £45,000 inheritance.

Her bill looks as follows:

AMY'S TAX BILL (£45,000 INHERITANCE)

Amount	Tax Rate	Amount Payable
£12,370	Exempt	No Tax
The next £10,000	@ 20%	£2,000
Remaining £22,630	@ 30%	£6,789
Total CAT Bill		£8,789
Plus Probate Bill		none
Final Tax Bill		**£8,789**

Note: If either party pays the deposit and/or most of the mortgage, and the house is in joint names, the other may be deemed to have taken a "gift" of the entire property.

To cater for this future tax bill, Mark and Amy take out a Section 60 policy on a "joint life, first death" basis. It has a "sum assured" (promised payout) of £40,000. They choose an index-linked policy to keep pace with inflation, and a large sum to cover any increase in property values and/or taxes. Money left over will just go into the estate; it won't go to waste.

PASSING ON A FAMILY BUSINESS

Business & Agricultural Reliefs

You can pass on a family business or farm to your son or daughter with virtually no tax charge. The 1997/98 Budget boosted the percentage of *qualifying* business assets exempt from CAT to 90 per cent. Agricultural property also qualifies for this relief, but the beneficiary who inherits the property must be a *farmer*. This is determined not by their occupation, but by the assets they own.

A son or daughter, can inherit business/agricultural assets worth £1.8 million, without paying CAT, but the exemption thresholds are much lower for more distant relatives.

The relief can also be clawed back if the assets are not held for at least ten years. Get expert advice.

Handling Succession

Passing on a family business is not just about tax. It intrudes into many delicate areas; family politics, power, your own financial and personal needs. Research by BDO Simpson Xavier's family business unit shows that only 24 per cent of businesses survive the first generation; 14 per cent make it beyond the third.

Here are some tips:

- Take a structured approach to succession planning. Don't be overcome by events.

- Start planning early.

- Think hard about who you want to run the business. To ensure that it ends up in the right hands, you may need to favour one heir — your successor.

- Discuss your plans with this person, and the rest of the family. You want them to support this person, too.

- Minimise estate taxes through the use of lifetime gifts and trust settlements. You can use Section 60 policies to foot any remaining tax bill.

- Consider insurance to compensate others.

Source: Philip Smyth, a family business counsellor with BDO Simpson Xavier.

TIP: Even a modest inheritance can turn a young head. If you want to stop children from squandering an inheritance — the so-called "Porsche syndrome" — consider setting up a discretionary trust. See Chapter 14. "Children", p. 138.

A LIVING WILL

Ever worried about who will manage your finances if you succumb to Alzheimer's or another wasting illness? You can make a "Living Will" which maps out how you and your money will be looked after, thanks to the Powers of Attorney Act 1996. You can nominate who will look after you and your affairs when you get ill, but agree costs and other fine points beforehand. Get more details from a trusted solicitor.

FUNERAL COSTS

This is another, sometimes overlooked, part of planning for death. Some people even like sorting out their funeral arrangements well in advance — especially the service!

A no-frills funeral costs £1,500-£2,000, but the fee rises to £3,500 if you pick an expensive plot and lots of "extras". Taking a shared plot with your spouse or family members will cut the cost. Cremation is the cheapest option, starting at around £200 for the cremation fee, urn and certificate.

You can organise your finances in different ways. At least one Dublin-based undertaker's has a "pre-paid funeral" plan that lets you organise and pay in advance. Some people scale down an existing life assurance policy; others take out low-cost life plans especially for their funeral.

CONCLUSION

Most of us avoid making a will, taking out life assurance — in short, doing anything that reminds us of our mortality. That's only natural, but good financial planning is a matter of life *and* death. Here are four good reasons for dealing with inheritance planning, before it's too late:

- You can provide for family, friends and charities

- It brings peace of mind (usually)

- You, or your family, will pay less tax

- Hard-earned wealth — like a family business — is less likely to be squandered.

24

Widowhood

"Only I can make the journey, that others made before me."

Rupert Strong (1911–1984) — Psychoanalyst, poet,
from Monkstown, Dublin

Losing a husband to death is deeply traumatic, whether you are aged 45 or 85. If you are cohabiting, with no marriage certificate, legal problems and the lack of social supports can make it even tougher.

This chapter offers some advice on how to organise your financial affairs before and after a bereavement. Topics are listed below. Funeral costs are covered in Chapter 23, "Inheritance Planning", p. 241, and Making a Will on p. 85

• Paperwork	p. 243
• Life assurance policies	p. 244
• Family home	p. 244
• Pensions, Social Welfare	p. 245
• More Help	p. 246

NOTE: If you were not married to your partner, see p. 122 Try to plan ahead while both of you are alive and well.

FINANCIAL MATTERS

The Early Days

Avoid big financial decisions just after your spouse's death, like whether to sell the family home. Other "housekeeping" tasks, like accessing bank accounts and claiming on life assurance policies, must be tackled sooner.

This will be easier if your husband's documents are in order. Try to keep life policies, bank books, etc., together *and* in an accessible place. Tell your spouse where they are. Leave them with the family solicitor or in a bank safe if you worry about security. Keep a will in a fire-proof container — if possible.

If vital paperwork is missing, contact your husband's bank or solicitor. Family members or trusted friends may also know where the documents are.

The Will

Chapter 23 describes what happens if a person dies with or without a will.

A wife can only be "cut out" of a will, or disinherit her husband, in certain circumstances. For example, if you or your partner was guilty of a criminal offence or had deserted the other spouse for at least two years previously. You can waive your succession rights voluntarily, or they can be *extinguished* by a court if you get a Judicial Separation or divorce. If you or your husband change a will, tell each other. Advance warning can avoid shocks — and huge tax bills.

WARNING: If there is no will, a surviving partner automatically inherits two-thirds of their spouse's estate. The rest is divided equally among the children. So, if your husband dies *intestate*, and the house was in his sole name, you may not inherit all of it. You may also be liable for Capital Acquisitions Tax (CAT) p. 236 if your children "gift" their share to you.

Life Assurance

Contact your insurance broker, or life company, if you think your husband had a life assurance policy but you can't find it. His name, date of birth and address should be enough to verify its existence. You can still claim a payout, if the document is missing, but you must give some documentary proof.

See also the section on Pension below, for *"death in service"* gratuity.

Bank Accounts

If you had a *joint* bank account on which either of you could sign cheques, you can draw on it immediately. This money is yours, and will not go into your husband's estate.

If the account is held in your partner's sole name and you need money urgently, contact your solicitor. The bank should be able to arrange an *executor's overdraft*, or an *administrator's overdraft*, which is really a loan on the money in the estate.

If there is a substantial sum in the account — over £5,000, for example — the bank manager may ask for a *Grant of Probate* or *Letters of Administration* for authorisation to release the funds. This happens when the estate is already being divided up.

The Family Home

A house held in *joint* names should pass to the surviving spouse when the first partner dies. If you have a life assurance protection policy, an outstanding mortgage will be paid off. These policies haven't always been obligatory, so ask your lender (bank or building society) if you have one. Do this when you are both still alive, preferably, and take out a policy if necessary. Make sure it is payable on *first*, not *second*, death. In the latter case, the mortgage won't be cleared until *both* spouses die.

If there is no mortgage, make sure the deeds of the house are kept in a safe place. This is your record of title to the property.

> TIP: Don't rush into selling the family home. Try to wait — perhaps a couple of years — before making such a big decision.

Pension

If your spouse belonged to a company or public sector pension scheme, you can probably claim a pension. This right sometimes extends to partners in long-standing "live-in" relationships, be they heterosexual or gay. But that's rare.

If your spouse was a public-sector worker, you should be entitled to a *death-in-service* gratuity — usually a multiple of their par salary, paid as a lump sum. You can also apply for a *contributory widow's pension* from the Department of Social Welfare, whatever your age. The maximum rate will be £71.10 from June, but this is based on the PRSI record of you or your husband. You can work and still draw this, but it may be taxed. Sadly, many women never claim their husbands' pensions, though they are entitled to if he or they have sufficient PRSI credits. Moreover, these pensions are paid *regardless* of the woman's age.

Company pension schemes vary enormously. You may be entitled to a death-in-service benefit, if the scheme provides one, but a spouse's pension is not usually paid until 65. Contact the scheme's trustees about this. The scheme's rules will also determine how much you get, and when you are paid. In general, your pension will be one-third or half of your deceased husband's entitlement. If you have children, they may be entitled to a payment, too.

What if your husband had retired? Most life company annuities guarantee the pension for five years after the scheme member dies. If your husband dies six months after retirement, you get his full pension for the guaranteed period. If he bought a *joint life annuity*, with the lump sum from his pension fund, you are entitled to a pension until you die. If he didn't, your company pension will dry up when the guaranteed period ends.

Tax and Social Welfare Benefits

A surviving spouse (widow or widower) can qualify for extra tax reliefs and social welfare benefits. In the year of bereavement, you can claim a widowed person's allowance of £5,800 (1997/98), which is twice the single person's rate. In the following year, it shrinks to £3,900. You can claim an extra allowance if you have dependent children.

These allowances should cut your tax bill — if some of your income is taxable — because they raise your tax-free income threshold.

If your income is small, you may qualify for a widow's non-contributory pension. This will be £67.50 per week from June 1997, (£72.50 if aged 80 or more). Ask at your local Social Welfare office.

Sharing Roles

Ideally, you should discuss pension, tax and inheritance issues with your husband before he dies. Shielding a spouse from financial matters does them no favour. At worst, you may never get the life assurance payout your husband had planned for you — or vice versa.

If one spouse controls the budget and bank accounts, the other can be doubly traumatised when widowhood forces them to start making independent financial decisions. Sharing responsibilities and planning ahead can spare a lot of pain.

More Help

You can get advice and valuable support from several groups. These include the National Widows' Association, 12 Upper Ormond Quay, Dublin 7 (Tel: (01) 677 0977), the Retirement Planning Council, 27–29 Pembroke Street Lr., Dublin 2, (Tel: (01) 661 3139) or the Bereavement Counselling Service Office, Dublin Street, Baldoyle, Co. Dublin (Tel: (01) 839 1766). The latter only gives counselling on dealing with grief, not financial affairs.

CONCLUSION

Death is a painful experience but, like many others, we can learn from it. A widow who takes charge of her own life may even feel a stronger person as a result. Moreover, she can boost her income by claiming all her due entitlements.

This book aims to help all women — whatever their age or marital status — make clear, informed, decisions about financial issues that affect them. Money *does* matter, especially when your future and your family's future, are at stake.

Appendix

A. USEFUL ADDRESSES

Business links

First Step*
Eglington Road
Dublin 4
Tel: (01) 260 0988

County/City Enterprise Boards**
c/o: Department of Enterprise & Employment
Tel: (01) 661 4444

National Federation of Business and Professional Women's
Clubs of the Republic of Ireland
President: Lois Tobin
Carrick, 42 Upper Newcastle
Galway
Tel: (091) 524329

Network***
The Organisation for Women in Business
19 Whitehall Road
Terenure, Dublin 12
Tel: (01) 455 6628

*Grant-aids new businesses that would not qualify for bank loans or
        other finance
**Give similar help, at regional level
***Network holds regular functions, has a members' directory etc.

Legal Advice

Free Legal Advice Centres (FLAC)
(Voluntary)
49 South William Street
Dublin 2
Tel: (01) 679 4239

Legal Aid Board
(State-run)
Earlsfort Terrace
St Stephen's Green House
Dublin 2
Tel: (01) 661 5811

Marriage Breakdown

Accord
(formerly Catholic Marriage Advisory Council)
39 Harcourt Street
Dublin 2
Tel: (01) 478 0866

AIM
(Family law information, mediation and counselling centre)
6 D'Olier Street
Dublin 2
Tel: (01) 670 8363

Divorce Action Group
54, Middle Abbey Street
Dublin 1
Tel: (01) 872 7395

Family Mediation Service
(State-run)
5th floor, Irish Life Centre
Lower Abbey Street
Dublin 1
Tel: (01) 872 8277

Gingerbread
(Voluntary advice and support group for one-parent families)
29 Dame Street
Dublin 2.
Tel: (01) 671 0291

Professional Groups

Association of Secondary Teachers in Ireland (ASTI)
Winetavern Street
Dublin 8
Tel: (01) 671 9144

Irish Federation of University Teachers
11 Merrion Square
Dublin 2
Tel: (01) 661 0910

Irish National Teachers' Organisation (INTO)
35 Parnell Square
Dublin 1
Tel: (01) 872 2533

Irish Nurses Organisation (INO)
11 Fitzwilliam Place
Dublin 2
Tel: (01) 676 0137/8

Training

Employment Equality Agency
36, Upper Mount Street
Dublin 2
Tel: (01) 662 4577

Irish National Organisation of the Unemployed (INOU)
6, Gardiner Row
Dublin 1
Tel: (01) 878 8635

FAS, (Training & Employment Authority)
27 Upper Baggot Street
Dublin 4
Tel: (01) 668 5777

New Opportunities for Women
(NOW)
32 Upper Fitzwilliam Street
Dublin 2
Tel: (01) 661 5268

Voluntary/Advice Agencies

Threshold (mortgage/rent problems)
Head Office
Church Street, Dublin 7
Tel: (01) 872 6311
or
8 Fr Matthew Quay, Cork
Tel: (021) 271250
or
Ozanan House
St Augustine Street, Galway
Tel: (091) 63080

FISC (Financial Information Service Centres)
87–89 Pembroke Road
Dublin 4
Tel: (01) 668 2044

Money Advice Budgeting Service (MABS)
See: Local phone book or, c/o Department Social Welfare
Tel: (01) 874 8444

Society of St Vincent de Paul
Head Office
8 New Cabra Road
Dublin 7
Tel: (01) 838 4164

Women's Groups

Irish Countrywomen's Association
58, Merrion Road
Dublin 4
Tel: (01) 668 0453

National Association of Widows in Ireland
12, Upper Ormond Quay
Dublin 7
Tel: (01) 677 0977

National Women's Council of Ireland
32, Upper Fitzwilliam Street
Dublin 2
Tel: (01) 661 5268

Irish Federation of Women's Clubs
11 St. Peter's Road
Phibsboro
Dublin 7
Tel: (01) 868 0080

Women in the Home
c/o 12 Springfield Road
Templeogue
Dublin 6W
Tel: (01) 490 6778

Zonta International (worldwide association of
executive & professional women)
c/o Audrey Lawler
41 Cecil Street
Limerick
Tel: (061) 419414

B. SOCIAL WELFARE

Social Welfare payments fall into two main categories.

Benefits are not means-tested, and are based on your PRSI contribution record or an automatic entitlement — such as child benefit. If you have been in regular employment and have a long PRSI payment record, you may be entitled to extra benefits.

Allowances are means-tested. You may qualify for the full payment if your income is below a certain level, or you may get a part-payment. You may also qualify for other benefits, like a free fuel allowance or butter vouchers, if you are receiving social assistance (non-PRSI-based) payments or are over 66 and getting a Social Welfare pension. Your local Health Board officer can make extra, discretionary payments.

Many people never claim all the Social Welfare payments they are entitled to. Your local Social Welfare office or Citizens' Information Centre (see phone directory) can tell you which of the following payments you may qualify for:

Non-Means-Tested

CHILD BENEFIT (£ INCREASE FROM 1/9/97)

Number of Children	Monthly Allowance	
	1996/97	1997/98#
1	£29	£30
2	£58	£60
3	£92	£99
4	£126	£138
5	£160	£177
6	£194	£216
7	£228	£255
8	£262	£294

DESERTED WIFE'S BENEFIT

	1996/97	1997/98
Maximum	£68.10 per week	£71.10 per week
Each Dependent Child	£17 per week	£17 per week

WIDOW'S/WIDOWER'S CONTRIBUTORY PENSION

	1996/97	1997/98
Maximum	£68.10 per week	£71.10 per week
Each Dependent Child	£17 per week	£17 per week

DISABILITY/UNEMPLOYMENT BENEFIT

	1996/97	1997/98
Adult	£64.50 per week	£67.50 per week
Each Dependent Child	£13.20 per week	£13.20 per week

Means-Tested

ONE-PARENT FAMILY PAYMENT

	1996/97	1997/98
Adult	£64.50 per week	£67.50 per week
Each Dependent Child	£15.20 per week	£15.20 per week

WIDOW'S AND WIDOWER'S NON-CONTRIBUTORY PENSION

	1996/97	1997/98
Adult	£64.50 per week	£67.50 per week
Dependent child? Claim the One-Parent Family payment instead		Widowers can claim pension from Oct. 1997

DESERTED, SEPARATED, PRISONERS WIFE'S ALLOWANCE

	1996/97	1997/98
Adult Dependent child? Claim One-Parent Family payment instead	£64.50 per week	£67.50 per week

UNEMPLOYMENT ASSISTANCE (SHORT TERM)

	1996/97	1997/98
Adult	£62.40 per week	£65.40 per week
Each Dependent Child	£13.20 per week	£13.20 per week

UNEMPLOYMENT ASSISTANCE (LONG TERM)

	1996/97	1997/98
Adult	£64.50 per week	£67.50 per week
Each Dependent Child	£13.20 per week	£13.20 per week

FUEL ALLOWANCE

	1996/97	1997/98
Mid-October to Mid-April	£5 per week	£5 per week

RENT ALLOWANCE

Paid by Health Board	Discretionary

MEDICAL CARD

Provided by Health Board (see p. 73)	Free hospital accommodation, medicines, and GP service

Note: The 1997/98 increases will apply from June 1997, with the exception of child benefit. People aged over 66 or 80, and those with adult dependants can claim higher payments.

FAMILY INCOME SUPPLEMENT (FIS)

This can boost your take-home pay significantly, without affecting your entitlement to a medical card. Lone parents in full-time employment can qualify for FIS too. To qualify, you must:

- Be working at least 19 hours a week full-time employment

- Be maintaining a child aged under 18, or aged between 18 and 22 in full-time education

- Have gross weekly earnings below a certain threshold, less PRSI and levies (from June 1997)

FIS is paid once a week by means of a book of payable orders which can be cashed at your post office. The size of the payment depends on the number of children you have and your income. From June, if you have one child, and earn £140 per week (before tax), for example, your FIS payment will be 60 per cent of the difference between £205, which is your FIS income threshold (see table below), and £140. That means £39 per week, or £2,028 per year.

From June 1997, the FIS thresholds will be raised as follows:

Family Size	Increase	New Income Limit
1 child	£10	£205
2 children	£10	£225
3 children	£10	£245
4 children	£10	£265
5 children	£10	£290
6 children	£10	£310
7 children	£10	£327
8 children	£10	£344

If you are living with a partner, whether you are married or not, his income will be assessed when calculating your FIS payment. If you pay PRSI (income over £80) or levies (income over £197) you will get further additions.

SIGNING ON THE LIVE REGISTER

This was a big issue in 1996, thanks to a campaign by the National Women's Council of Ireland and the INOU. To "sign on", you must be "unemployed, available for work and genuinely seeking work". You are no longer on the "Live Register" if you have been out of work for two years, and have not claimed an unemployment or disability payment.

There are two types of payment: Unemployment Benefit (UB) and Unemployment Assistance (UA). To get UB, you must have:

- 39 weeks PRSI paid, and

- 39 weeks PRSI paid or credited in the relevant tax year. For example, if you wish to claim UB in 1997, the relevant tax year is 6 April 1995 to 5 April 1996.

UA is based on a means test.

If you are unemployed, you should contact your local Social Welfare office to apply for UA or UB, on the first day you stop working. You may be disqualified for UA or UB for up to nine weeks if you:

- Lose your job through your own misconduct

- Leave of your own free will

- Refuse an offer of suitable work, do not look for work and/or refuse (without good reason) to attend a FAS course

- Are made redundant, and receive a redundancy payment of more than £15,000 *and* are aged under 55.

When making your first claim for UA or UB, bring identification, such as a full driver's licence or passport. Many women cannot sign on the live register, because of child care duties, but this can exclude you from certain payments and training opportunities. If this happens to you, contact the INOU and/or the National Women's Council of Ireland (see Appendix A).

C. MOTOR MILEAGE RATES (APPROVED CIVIL SERVICE)

These rates are used to reimburse employees who use their cars in the course of work.

Inclusive Rate per Mile	Engine Capacity		
Official Mileage in a Year	Under 1138 cc	1138 cc–1387 cc	1388 cc +
	p	p	p
Up to 2,000	49.87	57.70	68.20
2,001–4,000	54.98	62.98	75.79
4,001–6,000	29.44	33.38	37.84
6,001–8,000	27.74	31.35	35.31
8,001–12,000	24.33	27.30	30.26
12,001 +	20.92	23.25	26.27

D. GRANTS FOR WOMEN'S GROUPS

The Department of Social Welfare gives grant support for groups involved in voluntary and community work. These include those run for, or on behalf of, women, such as:

- The community development programme

- Voluntary organisations

- Locally-based women's groups

- Projects which tackle the problems of moneylending and indebtedness

- Groups assisting lone parents who are returning to the workforce, or are taking up "second-chance" education

- Special once-off grants are also provided.

Contact the Department of Social Welfare's Voluntary and Community Services Section, Floor Five, Áras Mhic Dhiarmada, Store Street, Dublin 1. Tel: (01) 874 8444, extension 3827 or 3864. Or, ring your local Social Welfare office or the Department's information service, at (01) 874 8444.

The Department of Health (01) 671 4711 may assist groups which provide respite care for others.

E. YOUR RIGHTS UNDER THE PENSIONS ACT (1990)

The Pensions Act is a key piece of legislation. It gives you — the pension scheme member — important rights. These include:

- The Right of Information

- The Right to Funding Data

- The Right to a "Portable Pension".

- The Right to Elect Member Trustees.

The Right to Information

You are entitled to information about the way in which the scheme is structured, the benefits it provides and how the investment is performing. However, you have to request most of this information, as you will not get it automatically.

For example, you are entitled to see the documents which set up the pension scheme, including the trust deeds, the scheme rules and any changes to them. You can also get a benefits statement which confirms your retirement age, the size of your premium contributions, value of your fund to date and additional benefits (life-assurance cover) in the pension scheme. You may have to request these documents.

Your trade union automatically gets an annual report for the scheme and, in the case of pension schemes on a defined-benefit basis with 50 or more members audited annual accounts. The annual accounts reveal if the pension scheme has "self-invested", in other words lent money to the parent company, in excess of 5 per cent of the scheme resources. You can ask for a copy of both.

The Right to Funding Data

Trustees of defined-benefit funded schemes must submit actuarial funding certificates to the Pensions Board every three-and-a-half years. These confirm that there are sufficient assets in the fund to meet its current liabilities. For the purpose of calculating these assets "self-investment" or concentration of investment in excess of certain percentages is excluded.

As a pension scheme member, you are entitled to get this information, but you have to ask for it. Your trade union automatically gets this information in the annual report for the scheme.

The Right to a "Portable" Pension

Thanks to the 1990 legislation, pensions are far more mobile and you don't have to lose benefits when you change jobs. See section "When You Leave your Job" below for more details.

For further information about your rights, contact the Pensions Board, Holbrook House, Holles Street, Dublin 2; Tel: (01) 676 2622.

HOW BIG A LUMP SUM CAN YOU TAKE?

Years of Service to Retirement	Max. Lump Sum as a Fraction of Final Pensionable Salary
1–8	3/80ths for each year
9	30/80ths for each year
10	36/80ths for each year
11	42/80ths for each year
12	48/80ths for each year
13	54/80ths for each year
14	63/80ths for each year
15	72/80ths for each year
16	81/80ths for each year
17	90/80ths for each year
18	99/80ths for each year
19	108/80ths for each year
20	120/80ths for each year

The Right to Elect Member Trustees

The trustees of a pension scheme have an important job, because they police the running of the scheme. They also have access to key information and are responsible for paying out benefits from the scheme.

Employees who belong to schemes with 50 or more members have the right to elect at least two member trustees. But this right must be sought by a trade union representing at least 50 per cent of active members of the pension scheme, or at least 15 per cent of the scheme's qualifying members (pensioners and active members) or by the employer.

When You Leave Your Job

In the past, people who left their jobs also had to leave valuable pension rights behind them. Now, thanks to the Pensions Act, your pension is far more "portable".

Under Five Years

If you have been with a company for less than five years, you have full access to your own pension contributions. The typical options available to you are as follows:

- Take a cash refund of your contributions, including AVCs. Tax will be deducted at 25 per cent, however

or

- Leave the value of your contributions in the scheme. These will be paid to you as a pension at your normal retirement date. This is called a "deferred pension". The drawback is that this sum will be frozen in money terms at the date you leave your job, and not revalued between then and your retirement date, unless the scheme rules provide otherwise

or

- Transfer the gross amount of your contributions into a new company pension plan with your new employer or, alternatively, into a personal retirement bond with an insurance company.

You can never take a refund of the contributions made by your employer to the scheme on leaving service. However, some schemes give "vested rights" after a minimum period of service, usually five or ten years. This means that you are entitled to a deferred pension based on both your own and your employer's contributions which you can continue to hold in the scheme or, if the scheme rules permit, can transfer to a new company scheme or a personal retirement bond with an insurance company.

Over Five Years

After five years you are entitled to "preserved benefits" under the Pensions Act. This means that if you leave a scheme before retirement date, having five years' service (at least two of which were after 1 January 1991), you have the following choices:

- Preserve the benefits you have built up after 1 January 1991 in the scheme you are leaving. The way in which your preserved benefit is calculated depends on whether you are a member of a defined benefit or a defined contribution scheme. If it is a defined benefit scheme, the formula is as follows:

  Your preserved benefit is calculated as the "long-service benefit". That is, a pension expectation at normal retirement age multiplied by the reckonable service (i.e. the period of your scheme membership, which is not necessarily the whole period of employment, and excluding any time when covered for death benefits only), after 1 January 1991. This is divided by the number of years of reckonable service to normal pension age, including service before 1 January 1991. Preserved benefits granted under a defined benefit scheme will be revalued every year, starting from 1 January 1996, until the benefits become payable on retirement.

  The situation is much simpler for a defined contribution scheme. The preserved benefit is the accumulated value of contributions paid by you, and on your behalf, after 1 January 1991, or the date you started work, if later.

or

- Transfer your preserved benefits to your new employer's scheme.

    or

- Transfer these benefits to an approved insurance policy or contract.

If you qualify for preserved benefits, you cannot get a refund of any contributions paid after 1 January 1991. This also applies to AVCs. However, you can get a cash refund (minus 25 per cent tax) of contributions paid before that date.

Moving jobs can be stressful enough, without the added worry of sorting out your pension benefits. Contact the Pensions Board (Tel: (01) 676 2622) or the pension scheme's broker if you need advice. You can also get a copy of the Pension Board's leaflet, "What Happens to My Pension If I Leave?"

Note: Information for this section was provided by the Pensions Board.

Glossary

Additional Voluntary Contributions (AVCs): can be used to "top up" (increase) premium payments into a pension fund, to maximise tax relief. Can be paid as a lump sum, or in regular instalments.

Annual Percentage Rate (APR): total cost of credit including charges, expressed as an annual percentage of the amount of credit given.

annuity: annual payment which a life company agrees to pay you in return for a lump sum. Also called a pension.

Automated Teller Machine (ATM): popular term is the "hole in the wall" machine, or cash dispenser. This is a terminal, located in public places and inside banks, which allows you to make transactions on your bank/building society account, with a plastic ATM card.

bid price: price at which "units" are sold in a unit-linked fund. They are bought back by the company at the "offer" price. Typically, there is a 5 per cent difference in these prices. This is the "bid offer spread".

broker: person who acts as an agent or go-between when buying or selling financial products or services. Note: An "independent" broker should represent at least five insurance companies.

Business Expansion Scheme (BES): this allows 48 per cent taxpayers to claim full tax relief on approved BES investment projects. This facility was extended for three years in the 1996 Budget. Section 35 film investments qualify for similar relief.

charge card: like a credit card, can be used to buy goods and services on credit. However, it does not offer a "revolving" credit facility, and your bill must be settled in full when the statement arrives.

commission: sum of money paid to insurance intermediary — i.e. broker/agent/tied agent — in return for business sold by that person.

Compound Annual Return (CAR): reflects the true return (before tax) on a savings/deposit account, allowing for the rolling up of interest.

credit: use of someone else's funds — e.g. bank or department store — in exchange for promise to repay, usually with interest, at a later date.

credit card: allows you to buy goods/services on credit, subject to limits and rules set by the company (usually a bank) that issued the card.

death-in-service benefit: payment made if you die in employment, usually by a pension scheme to your dependants.

debit card: this is a plastic card that works like an electronic "cheque". It allows money to be deducted directly from your bank account to pay for goods or services.

direct debit: instruction from a customer to their bank to debit their account with a sum of money (fixed or variable) to pay another party. It is often used to pay bills.

Dublin Inter-Bank Offer Rate (DIBOR): a "wholesale" rate quoted on the "interbank" market where banks lend surplus cash to each other. Commercial loans sometimes expressed as DIBOR plus $x\%$.

hire purchase: literally, a combination of hiring and purchasing. You have the use of goods — but do not own them — while paying for them. Ownership automatically transfers with the last payment.

leasing: a method of obtaining the use of a large asset — usually a car or office machinery — in return for regular payments. In car leasing, you can often arrange to purchase the vehicle at the end of the lease agreement. You may have to pay an extra cash sum, however.

life assured: the person whose life is covered by an assurance policy.

maturity: the life expectancy of a loan from the date when it is taken out to the last repayment date.

mortgage: a loan provided for buying a home or any other property.

security: assets like a house, life-assurance policies and other items, which are pledged to support a loan.

self-administered scheme: a special pension arrangement for company directors, whereby they can invest in Revenue-approved assets (outside the life-assurance industry) and still qualify for zero tax on any pension-fund profits.

standing order: an instruction from a customer to their bank to make a regular payment (often monthly) from their account. It is often used to arrange mortgage repayments.

sum assured: the amount of cover that you have on a life policy.

term assurance: a life-insurance policy which is taken out for a specified period and guarantees to pay a lump sum if the policyholder dies within that time. "Convertible" term assurance permits you to extend or otherwise change the original policy.

unit-linked fund: a life-assurance investment. Premiums paid by thousands of investors are "pooled" and used by a "fund manager" to trade in assets, in the hopes of making a profit.

"whole of life" assurance: a life-assurance policy which gives policy-holders permanent cover on their lives. It does not have to be renewed, unlike term assurance, but is a lot more expensive.

"with profits" policy: a life-assurance investment which pays the policy-holder a return that is related to the profits earned by that life company. Profits are added through the annual bonus and a final — terminal — bonus. Once added, they cannot be taken away.

NOTE: This glossary is largely drawn from three sources:

Banking in Ireland, Irish Banks' Information Service.

"Fact File", the Irish Insurance Federation.

"The Way We Talk", Irish Life staff training document.

Index